HOME
HORTICULTURE

HOME HORTICULTURE

ROBERT J. BAUSKE
Iowa State University

WEST PUBLISHING COMPANY

ST. PAUL · NEW YORK · LOS ANGELES · SAN FRANCISCO

Copyright © 1976 By WEST PUBLISHING CO.
All rights reserved
Printed in the United States of America

Library of Congress Cataloging in Publication Data
Bauske, Robert J.   1921–
   Home horticulture
   Includes index
   1. Gardening. I. Title
SB453.B393   635   76–2733
ISBN 0–8299–0112–4
2nd Reprint—1978

PREFACE ─────────────────────────────────

The purpose of this book is twofold: to acquaint you with the way plants grow; and to help you select and grow plants of all types in and around your home. We hope to accomplish this painlessly; but if the technical information is too difficult, the later chapters on specific types of plants and their care can still be useful.

Horticulturists are the people you call florists, nurserymen, turf growers, orchardists, or vegetable growers. In fact, all plant growers except foresters and those farmers who raise only "field" crops (corn, oats, soybeans) are considered horticulturists. Horticultural tasks vary from pulling weeds in your vegetable garden to excising a few cells from the tip of a plant's stem and growing them in a test tube on special chemicals.

Horticulture changes, however, and to keep up you will need to read about the changes. This can be done by reading magazines devoted to the subject, such as *Flower and Garden* or *Horticulture*, or by joining the American Horticultural Society or a plant or flower club. New books are also available in local libraries.

We want to lead you through home horticulture from the basic principles involved in plant growth to propagation, to container growing, and finally to designing your own landscape. And you should be able to maintain those landscape plants properly. You will see that horticulture is an art, and a science—and fun.

I would like to thank Burl Parks for the use of his landscape plans and James Wilson for the drawings. And for the endless hours of editing and proofreading, my sincere thanks to my wife, Grace.

*

CONTENTS

†

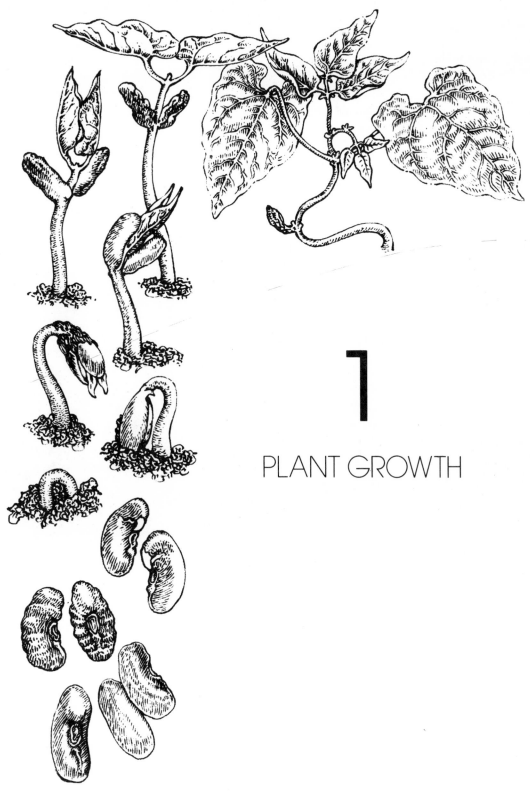

1

PLANT GROWTH

Plants are made up of cells. The embryonic plant in a seed arises from a single cell—the fertilized egg. The cells of the embryo divide and differentiate until an organism (the plant) composed of many different kinds of cells is produced. Differences in the arrangement and morphology of cells account for many of the variations within and between plants. Groups of cells are arranged together to form tissues. Some of these tissues are made up of actively dividing cells located at the tips of roots and stems. As they replicate and enlarge they cause elongation of the stems and roots. Similar tissues occur within stems and roots and their increase results in greater girth or thickness. These are called **meristematic** tissues. Those at the tips are **apical** meristematic tissues, and those causing thickening of stems and roots are cambial meristematic tissues—or just **cambium**. Other tissues are no longer dividing and are made up either of one kind of cell (simple) or several kinds functioning together (complex). Simple tissues are most prevalent. They contribute strength and storage space and substance to plants.

We are particularly interested in two complex tissues, the **xylem** and the **phloem**. Both are involved in the intimate processes of life in the plant. The xylem is made up of many tubelike cells. These cells die, and the ends open up to make long water-conducting vessels. Water that enters the roots of the plant moves upward through these tubes, which branch to bring water to all parts of the plant. Nearby and closely associated with the xylem is another set of tubelike cells called the phloem. In the phloem move dissolved carbohydrates essential for the formation of new cells and tissues. This material must be in solution to move to other plant parts. These two tissues, composed largely of vessel-like cells, are associated to form the **vascular system**, similar to our own circulatory system. This is a fine network which sustains the life and growth of most plants.

Tissues combine to form the more visible structures of the plant, such as roots, stems, leaves, flowers, and seeds (or fruits containing seeds). These structures we shall examine more closely. The root is a good starting point. Its primary function is the absorption of water and nutrients, but it may also be a storage organ. In plants like the sweet potato, so much food is stored in the root that it becomes swollen. (Not all enlarged roots are edible.) Another function of the roots of most plants is anchorage—roots help to hold plants in a stationary position.

Some plants form what are called **taproots**. A taproot may descend into the soil for many feet with only a few rather small lateral branch roots. The more common type of root system is called **fibrous**. It is made up of many branched and rebranched roots which generally do not penetrate the earth very deeply. By measuring the length of all the roots formed on some very extensive fibrous root systems, scientists have found that a single plant may have more than a mile of roots. Interestingly, there is no way to predict where a branch root will develop. Branch roots may form all on one side of the root, opposite one another, or irregularly.

At the tip of each root is an area of meristematic tissue producing new cells which eventually elongate and push the root tip farther into the soil. This new growth produces the movement that makes roots so efficient. They are a dynamic part of the plant, constantly moving into new areas or reinvading old areas of the soil where water and nutrients might be present. Back from the tip the cells stop growing and take a more or less final form; we call this **differentiation**. It is in this area that many of the outer cells of the root seem to stretch like elongated balloons to form **root hairs**. Although root hairs are large enough to be visible, they are seldom seen. Their presence, however, increases the surface area of the root by ten or twenty times. Most water absorption occurs through these structures. Old roots lose these hairs, which are very brittle and easily broken off, and become covered over with less absorptive cells. This means that roots must keep growing and producing new root hairs if efficient absorption of water is to continue; even an old tree must produce new rootlets to maintain itself.

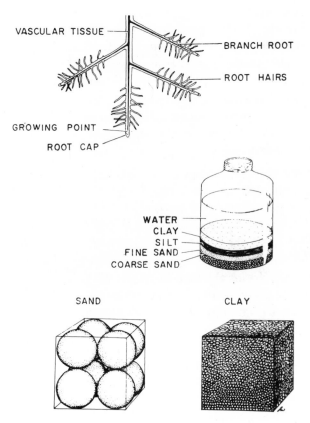

Root anatomy and environment

Plants usually are rooted in some fairly solid medium, like soil, but a few exceptions occur. Aquatic plants are adapted to growth in water. **Epiphytic** plants, capable of extracting moisture from the air, grow in crevices, rock, or tree crotches, with their roots exposed to the air (e. g., Spanish moss, some orchids). Most plants, however, grow best planted in soil-like substances. Let us examine such a medium.

Most soil is made of mineral materials that are simply remains of rocks which have been broken down by erosion or weathering. If you were to put a quarter cup of garden soil in a quart jar, add a pint of water, and mix it thoroughly, the mineral material would settle out in layers. The larger particles, sand, would drop down rapidly. A second layer of finer material, silt, would settle out next. It might take several days for the third layer of extremely fine particles, clay, to form. Anything still floating in the water would probably be organic matter. If all three mineral types and organic matter are present, you have the type of soil called loam.

Mineral particles determine the texture of the soil, and large concentrations of one type will alter the environment around the roots considerably. The water available to a plant is found mostly in the pore spaces—the spaces between soil particles. If the particles are large, as in sandy soil, the spaces between them are large, and water drains through quickly. Nutrients dissolved in the water are also drained away and become unavailable to the plants. However, such a soil in your garden may warm up quickly in the spring and it is easy to work. Conversely, the fine particles of a soil rich in clay produce small pores through which water moves with difficulty. This soil drains slowly and the pore spaces may remain filled with water. That might sound good, but roots must have air as well as water or they won't grow. A clay soil is difficult to work, slow to warm up, and, while it retains nutrients and water, provides little air.

Organic matter in the soil comes from plant and animal residues. It is generally in a state of decay and contains many microorganisms. Where humans do not intervene, the plant and animal materials are deposited, decay, and are taken up by plants, which are eaten by animals. The cycle works fairly well. But when people harvest the crop for eating or for display indoors, remove the weeds, and keep animals out of their gardens, the amount of organic matter (**humus**) becomes depleted.

Soil can be improved by adding organic matter. It is not possible to add too much. **Peat**, leaf mold, manure, compost, sawdust, and plant remains are some of the materials that can be used. Peat is the easiest to use because you can buy it at grocery stores, hardware stores, garden centers, and nurseries in big plastic bags which are lightweight and inexpensive. Moss peats like sphagnum or hypnum are best, but even the reedsedge peats are good. All of these are plant remains that were covered with water at one time and decomposed slowly and incompletely over many years. Their particle size is large compared to silt or clay, and each particle can absorb a large quantity of water. When mixed with soil, peat separates the soil particles, absorbs moisture, and eventually decomposes, releasing nutrients in the soil which the plants need for growth. By separating soil particles it improves drainage and allows air to penetrate to the pore spaces around the roots.

In addition to organic matter, fertilizer must be added to soils where rapid growth is desired or plan to remove part of the organic material (cut flowers, fruits, vegetables) or where we grow potted plants which constantly produce new tissues while being confined to a limited amount of soil. Additions of peat or fertilizer are called soil **amendments**. Plant growth can be improved by amending the soil. Fertilizers containing nutrients are usually available at garden centers, nurseries, or hardware stores. The essential nutrients for plants are nitrogen (N), phosphorus (P) and potassium (K). These are the elements the plant takes from the soil in largest quantities.

Other necessary elements such as calcium, magnesium, boron, molybdenum, chlorine, and zinc are usually present in sufficient quantities and seldom need replenishing in houseplant or garden soil.

Fertilizer bags generally indicate the amount of a specific element they contain by a series of numbers, a sort of code. If the numbers are 4-10-4, that means 4 percent of the weight of that bag is nitrogen (N), 10 percent is phosphorus (P), and 4 percent is potassium (K). The remaining material is inert carrier. So the N–P–K is 4-10-4. These elements are available to the plant as soon as they are in soil solution. (Interestingly, the bulk (94 percent) of the dry weight of a plant is made up of hydrogen (H) which comes from water, and carbon (C) and oxygen (O) from the air.)

The most critical soil constituents in mineral soils are organic matter and nitrogen. Both are usually present in small amounts but are lost through oxidation, leaching, or crop removal. Florists who grow crops in pots or benches with restricted amounts of soil generally make up soil mixtures to ensure good crop production. One of the most common mixtures is 1 part (by volume) soil, 1 part peat, and 1 part sand (or perlite or vermiculite). The soil is a safety reservoir containing some fertilizer; the peat helps hold moisture and nutrients while also aiding drainage and aeration; the sand improves drainage. Many florists eliminate soil and fertilize whenever they water plants.

So far we have been looking at the lower end of the plant and its environment. Now let's move up and examine the stem. Stems, as you are aware, may be upright or trailing or vining; they may grow above or below ground. (The white or Irish potato is an example of stem tissue found below ground. In this case it is a storage organ called a tuber.) Not all plants have an obvious stem. Many, like African violets, get along nicely without. Some people say the stem holds the leaves up in the light. That is apparently true but not essential. Probably all we can claim for the stem is that it serves as a bridge between the roots and the leaves. Xylem and phloem tissues are present throughout the stem and this vascular system branches to the leaves and flowers. The major types of stem

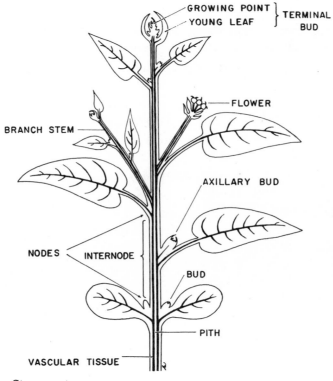

Stem anatomy

are **woody** and **herbaceous**. Woody stems are generally tougher; they often have bark around them and are usually capable of overwintering. Herbaceous stems are more succulent and are killed by cold temperatures. Their internal construction differs slightly from that of woody stems, but not enough to be of concern here.

At regular intervals along the stem you will find joints or markings from which the leaves or branches arise. These stem joints, called **nodes**, completely encircle the stem and include a general area a short distance above and below a leaf. They will be discussed later.

The angle formed by the leaf and the stem is called the **axil**. Buds which form there are called **axillary buds** (or lateral buds) to distinguish them from those at the tip (apex) of the stem, which are called apical or terminal buds.

Meristematic tissues abound in the nodal areas as well as at the shoot tips. This may lead to the development of branches or flowers and certainly to elongation. Additional meristematic tissue called cambium is associated with the vascular system and leads to an increase in girth of plant stems.

As we move on up the plant in our study, the leaf is the next major structure. Most leaves are composed of **blade** and **petiole**. The blade is the broad, flat, green area of the leaf. Leaf blades of cabbage and lettuce are the edible portions of those plants. Sometimes the blade is attached directly to the stem, but on most plants a thin stalk called a petiole extends between stem and blade. In celery and rhubarb, for example, the petiole is the important part because we use it as food, while the blades themselves are of little use. The petiole appears to continue into the blade. This extension is known as the **midvein** or midrib of the leaf. The vascular system of the stem branches out into the leaf by proceeding up the petiole to the midvein in the leaf blade where it branches and rebranches to form a network of secondary veins. Thus water which enters the roots is available to all the cells in the leaf.

The leaf has been partially waterproofed by nature with a waxlike coating called **cuticle**. There are some gaps or thin spots, but generally the cuticle coats the leaf evenly enough to prevent much direct water loss. It is formed by and covers the outer layer of cells called the **epidermis**. These cells, like your skin, act as a protective and containing layer. **Stomates** are natural openings which perforate both the epidermal layer and the cuticle. They are most abundant in the lower leaf surface and may appear there exclusively. Surrounding the stomates are guard cells

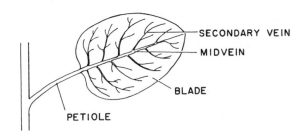

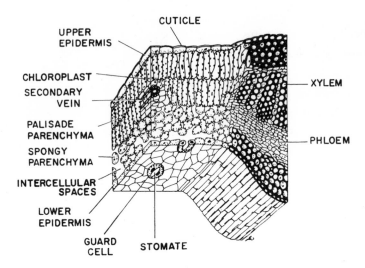

Leaf anatomy

which are capable of closing them under certain circumstances, such as absence of light or shortage of water.

Within the leaf blade are many simple, thin-walled cells (parenchyma). They are packed closely together in the upper half of the leaf blade (palisade parenchyma) and loosely fitted together near the lower surface (spongy parenchyma) so that the spaces between cells (intercellular spaces) are more obvious. Within all of the cells are organelles called **chloroplasts** containing the green pigment **chlorophyll**, which is of utmost importance to plants as well as to humans.

Green plants are able to manufacture carbohydrates (sugar or food) from raw materials taken from the soil and the air. This process is called **photosynthesis**. Humans and animals are all dependent upon photosynthesis—probably the most important chemical process known. All living organisms require energy, which they derive from the chemical energy of food consumed. Ultimately this leads back to plants, because while humans may consume animals for food, animals in turn must eat plants. Through plants the energy of the sun is trapped and made available to all living things.

Photosynthesis, which occurs mainly in the leaves of plants, can be represented by a chemical formula:

$$6CO_2 + 12H_2O \xrightarrow[\text{light}]{\text{chlorophyll}} 6H_2O + 6O_2 + C_6H_{12}O_6$$

This shows that in the leaf of a plant, carbon dioxide and water in the presence of chlorophyll and light are transformed into energy-rich carbohydrates (sugar). The chloroplasts are the factories in which the process takes place. In fact, it has been found that if a leaf is ground up, put in a water-filled test tube with carbon dioxide bubbled into this solution while shining a light on the tube, sugar will be formed in the tube. The green pigment chlorophyll is responsible for trapping the energy of light but will only do so within the choroplasts. If we extract chlorophyll pigment from the leaf without the chloroplasts and repeat our test tube experiment, no sugar will be formed.

Sunlight may be the energy source, but artificial light will also work. And in general, as we increase light intensity, we speed up the process of photosynthesis. Some plants require not much more than a lighted candle to begin sugar production; others must have a bright light. This is why some plants will grow in shaded locations and others must be planted in direct sunlight. Water for photosynthesis comes from the roots. Carbon dioxide enters through the stomates from the air around the leaf, which normally contains about 300 parts carbon dioxide per 1,000,000 parts of air (300 ppm). The oxygen formed escapes through the stomates and helps to sustain the level of oxygen in the atmosphere necessary for the continued existence of animal life. Temperature has little effect on the rate of photosynthesis.

The product of most interest to us is the sugar or carbohydrate. Production of this sugar is absolutely necessary for plant life—and, ultimately, for human life. What happens to it? Some is used in the plant as a building block. Combined with minerals absorbed from the soil, it becomes new cell walls or chlorophyll or any of the many compounds involved in the plant's structure. It may be used immediately in the cell in which it was formed, or it may move to some other part of the plant for use there or storage until needed. To move through the phloem sugar must be in solution. Sugar to be stored is generally converted into starch or oil. Enzymes are capable of performing this conversion in either direction. Not all of the sugar, however, is used this way. Some is used as an energy source. More about that later in a discussion of respiration.

Some photosynthesis may occur in green stems, but most occurs in the leaves. If insects or diseases destroy the leaves or parts of them, the potential food-manufacturing area of the plant is reduced. A plant allowed to wilt to the point of leaf loss may not have enough stored sugar to repair itself. Such plants may die or, at least, will have their growth reduced.

Another process which occurs in the leaves of plants is called **transpiration**. This is simply the loss of water in the form of vapor. With the stomates open there is direct movement of air into or out of the leaf. With that air may go water vapor. Should the air surrounding the leaf be low in relative humidity, the high relative humidity (96 to 98 percent) in the intercellular spaces within the leaf will allow moisture to escape rapidly to the outside. High relative humidity around the leaf will slow this water loss. Other factors affecting the transpiration rate are light, temperature, soil moisture content, and wind. Light is necessary for the opening of the stomates. At night the stomates close. This reduces transpiration 85 to 90 percent. Some moisture is also lost directly through the epidermal layers where gaps or thin spots occur in the cuticle. Higher temperatures increase the evaporation rate and raise the speed of transpiration. Lack of water in the soil causes the plant to wilt. Wilting automatically closes the stomates, reducing the rate of transpiration. Wind blowing over the leaf removes accumulated water vapor from around the stomates, effectively reducing the relative humidity on the outside of these openings. This increases the transpiration rate. However, that wind blowing across the leaf surface also cools the leaf, which reduces transpiration. So wind is a factor which may work to either increase or decrease transpiration. It depends upon the wind velocity and exposure of the plant to the wind.

Water and light are probably the two most important environmental resources for plant growth. We have already looked briefly at the use of light by plants. What about water? We have seen that it is an essential ingredient in photosynthesis. And anyone who has forgotten to water the garden or a house plant knows that a wilted plant is limp—lacking in turgor. Adding water to a wilted plant will allow it to recover its rigidity, unless you have waited too long.

Water entering the roots may contain soil minerals. In fact, those minerals are useless to the plant unless they are in solution, so water is essential for the absorption of soil minerals. Carbohydrates manufactured in the leaves must also be in solution to be transported through the phloem to other parts of the plant. Protoplasm, the living material in each cell, is largely water. In summary, water is absorbed as a liquid through the roots and moves upward in the xylem tubes of the vascular system. Some of it is used along the way as it rises to the leaves, where it escapes as a vapor.

More than 90 percent of the water which enters the roots escapes without being utilized by the plant. That seems wasteful. Why should plants need a constant source of water and then allow so much of it to pass through unused? The system must work. Some people have said that this movement of water helps to cool the plant like a radiator. Apparently this is true, but do plants need such a large amount of cooling? Scientists have discovered that water molecules have great tenacity. Water held in the xylem is confined to extremely narrow tubes. When water pressure at the top is reduced (transpiration), this negative force coupled with the tenacity of water molecules causes the entire column of water to rise. More water may then enter the base of the column. Apparently this loss of water helps pull water into the plant, making a continual upward movement of water. The process seems simple in terms of a glass tube or even a small plant. But it's difficult to imagine small columns of water starting in the roots of a redwood tree, moving fifty feet to the trunk, upwards one hundred and fifty feet, then out another fifty feet in a branch to a leaf. That, however, seems to be the system.

As mentioned earlier, some of the sugar formed during photosynthesis is a source of energy. Plants and animals use energy in the building and maintenance of protoplasm. This energy comes from the oxidation (burning) of organic compounds. The captured energy of light is released by means of this low-temperature burning of sugar (carbohydrate)—a process called **respiration**. In respiration a sugar is transformed into simpler substances with the release of energy. Respiration can be represented by the following chemical description:

$$C_6H_{12}O_6 + 6O_2 \longrightarrow 6CO_2 + 6H_2O + Energy$$

Some energy is lost as heat. Some is used in the movement of food through the plant, movement of chromosomes, and movement of roots. And some energy is used to convert food into cell walls and protoplasm.

Respiration occurs in all living cells, whether plant or animal, and it occurs in either the light or the dark. No pigment is necessary, but presumably the age and condition of the individual cells affects the rate of respiration. So long as sugar and oxygen are present in a living cell respiration will proceed. However, the process is quite temperature dependent. At very low temperatures little respiration occurs. As temperatures rise, the rate of respiration rises dramatically.

Within the plant a constant struggle between photosynthesis and respiration proceeds. Photosynthesis goes forward only in the light, but respiration occurs at night as well. Unless the plant can produce surplus sugar during the light period, respiration will use it up at night. Photosynthesis must exceed respiration for the plant to survive. When they are equal, the plant may live awhile but will have no reserve for repairs. This is called the **compensation point**.

Flowers are the reproductive parts of the plant. They develop into fruits containing seeds by which new generations are produced. Of course we grow plants for the beauty or fragrance of their flowers, but that is not why flowers exist. Even the most colorless, insignificant blooms, with or without pleasing fragrance, contain the same important parts as flowers that delight us with their esthetic qualities. If you have a flower at hand, see if you can find these parts.

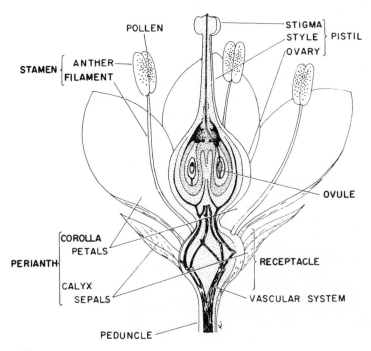

Flower anatomy

(The following description is of a typical or average flower; many modifications exist.) The stalk supporting the flower is the **peduncle**. The upper end of the peduncle is generally enlarged or swollen and is called the **receptacle.** Most of the flower parts seem to be attached to the receptacle. A series of green, pointed segments unite at the base of the flower forming a cuplike structure. The individual segments are **sepals** and the structure they form is a **calyx**. This is thought to be a protective device which surrounds the bud while the flower is developing. Sometimes the sepals are the color of the petals. The **petals** are the conspicuous, colorful part of the flower. Since they may contain nectar glands, it is the petals to which insects are apparently attracted. Collectively the petals are called the **corolla**. Calyx and corolla together are the **perianth**. Many flowers have no perianth (e. g., grasses), and others, such as poplars, oaks, and elms, have a greatly reduced perianth. The reproductive parts of the flower are the stamen and pistil. The **stamen** has pollen-bearing **anthers** supported on a long **filament**. When the **pollen** becomes mature, the anthers split open releasing the pollen. The stamen is the male part of the flower. The female part, the **pistil**, has an enlarged, ovule-bearing base called the **ovary** supporting an elongated **style** whose expanded tip is the **stigma**. The **ovule(s)** becomes the seed within the ovary, which becomes the fruit.

The flower we have described is called a **perfect** flower—both sexes are represented. But some plants have **imperfect** flowers in which only one sex is represented. They may be either staminate (male) or pistillate (female). A plant bearing staminate and pistillate flowers is said to be **monoecious**. Corn is a good example. The tassels are the male flowers and the ears are the female flowers. Other examples include birch, oak, elm, some cucumbers, and some begonias. There are also some plants which bear flowers of just one sex. Asparagus, cottonwood, bittersweet, and walnut are examples where the individual plant is either male or female. These are called **dioecious** plants.

We have said that flowers are the reproductive part of the plant. Actually the seeds formed in the flowers do the reproducing. We shall look at this entire process of seed formation. To begin with, why or how are flowers formed? Flowering, or floral induction, is a term representing a wide spectrum of morphological and physiological events. The most critical and least understood of these events is the transformation of a vegetative stem bud (meristem) into a floral bud. Why does that growing point quit producing stem and leaf tissue and begin producing flower parts? We don't have the full answer. At one time it was thought that when the ratio of carbon to nitrogen in the plant reached a certain point, flowering would be initiated. Most plant scientists discount that theory today. While we know a few things that initiate flowering in *some* plants, a complete explanation has not been found. Imagine, though, if we found some chemical that would induce flowering. We could produce flowers or fruit in great profusion for particular harvest dates simply by spraying that chemical on the plants. So far no such magic material has been discovered.

We do know that the length of the day or night will affect flowering in some plants. Traditionally we speak of "short-day" plants as those which will not flower unless the days become short, as they do in our latitude in the fall and winter. Actually, we now understand that it is the long, continued darkness and *not* the short day that produces the flowers. But when Garner and Allard first discovered this phenomenon in the early twentieth century, they thought that the short day was responsible, and we have kept that terminology. Plants like chrysanthemum and poinsettia will remain vegetative until the day length is reduced to less than twelve hours, and continued short days will allow flower buds to be initiated and developed. To prevent flowering of these plants, we have only to extend the light period artificially or interrupt the continuous darkness by turning lights on for a period in the middle of the night. On the other hand, if we wish to make chrysanthemums flower in the spring when the days are naturally long, we cover the plant with black cloth for at least thirteen hours starting in the evening. The plant is tricked into flowering because of artificially created short days. There are also long-day plants, such as tuberous begonias and some of the asters, which flower only when the day becomes long. Most plants are day neutral.

Temperature, too, affects flowering in some plants. The process is called **vernalization**. Usually a period of cold temperature is required before these plants will flower. Some varieties of wheat are planted in the fall, subjected to the cold temperatures of winter, and flower in the spring. The same varieties, if planted in the spring, would not get sufficient cold treatment and would fail to produce grain. Cabbage is an example of a plant which may receive enough cold in early summer to produce flowers when we would rather have it continue vegetative growth and not flower. This unwanted flowering is called "bolting." Biennial plants are essentially plants that require a cold period. They produce only foliage the first year; during the second growing season they produce more foliage, flower, and die. Without the cold winter to "vernalize" them they may not flower.

Alternate day-night temperatures also will increase the number of flowers on a few plants. For example, tomatoes grown at 80° F. in the daytime and 65° F. at night will produce far more flowers than if they had been grown at one unchanging temperature. **Thermal periodicity** is the name given to that phenomenon. Moisture apparently causes floral induction in another small group of plants, but little research has been conducted in this area. These are some of the bits and pieces to a puzzle that awaits final fitting together by scientists.

After floral induction, the next step is to produce seeds. For seeds to form, pollen has to reach the stigma. Even though seeds have been used to produce crops for thousands of years, it wasn't until the seventeenth century that an English naturalist observed pollination. Seeds were planted each season and flowers with their nectar and pollen attracted bees, but apparently no one saw any connection between the flowers and bees or the pollen and seeds.

Pollination is the mechanical process by which pollen reaches the stigma. This may occur by means of wind, rain, gravity, birds, animals, or insects. Much of the pollination in the garden occurs when insects are attracted to flowers by the color or odor, seek out nectar, and rub against the anthers in the process. As they struggle in the flower some pollen is rubbed off on the stigma. Or the insect may move to another flower on the same plant or a nearby similar plant and rub pollen off on that stigma.

One more step is necessary to produce viable seeds—**fertilization**. The pollen grain deposited on a stigma, whose surface usually becomes sticky when it is mature, now produces an elongating tube which penetrates the stigma and grows down the length of the style. When this tube reaches the ovary it enters an ovule. From the pollen grain a male gamete now passes down the pollen tube to the ovule where it is united with the female gamete, the egg. This union is called fertilization. The product is a **zygote** which eventually enlarges to become the embryo within the seed.

Once fertilization occurs the ovary usually begins to enlarge to form the fruit. In plants with many ovules in a single ovary, all ovules must be fertilized for the fruit to be well formed. If only a few are fertilized the fruit may be misshapen. Some varieties of oranges, grapes, and bananas will form fruit without fertilization, but the seeds in this fruit will not be viable. In those particular plants apparently pollination itself triggers some chemical action resulting in fruit formation.

In biological science seldom is any statement 100 percent true. Teaching must be at the 90 percent level. Most of the time things occur as they have been explained here but exceptions may be found to many of these statements.

GLOSSARY

Amendment: Material added to the soil, such as fertilizer or organic matter.

Anther: The part of the male sexual organ in a flower that produces the pollen.

Apical bud: The bud at the tip (or apex) of a stem.

Axil: The angle formed between the stem and upper side of the leaf.

Axillary bud: Bud that forms at the axil.

Blade: The broad, flat portion of the leaf.

Calyx: A cuplike structure composed of sepals, usually just below the petals, usually green.

Cambium: Layer of meristematic cells whose division results in increased girth of many plants.

Chlorophyll: The green pigment in plants essential to the photosynthetic process.

Chloroplast: Minute chlorophyll-containing structures in which photosynthesis takes place.

Compensation point: The point at which photosynthesis and respiration are equal.

Corolla: The part of the flower composed of petals.

Cuticle: A thin layer of waterproofing material, like wax, covering the epidermis.

Differentiation: The changes that occur in a cell from its formation until it reaches its final state of development.

Dioecious: A plant that produces either staminate or pistillate flowers but not both.

Epidermis: The outer layer of cells in the leaf, young stem, and root.

Epiphyte: A plant that grows on tree crotches or rock crevices and has its roots exposed to air.

Fertilization: The union of two gametes.

Fibrous root: Part of a network of branching roots all of which are similar in girth, in contrast to the taproot.

Filament: The stalk which supports the anther in a flower. It is part of the male sexual structure.

Herbaceous: Plants that have soft, nonwoody stems.

Humus: Organic matter in the soil that is partially decomposed.

Imperfect flower: A flower in which only one sex is represented; either a male flower or a female flower.

Meristematic: A type of plant tissue in which the cells are capable of continually dividing, never mature.

Midvein: A continuation of the petiole into the leaf blade; sometimes called a midrib.

Monoecious: A plant on which both staminate and pistillate flowers occur.

Node: An area around the stem where leaves and buds may occur.

Organic matter: Material that is or was living.

Ovary: The enlarged lower portion of the pistil.

Ovule: Enclosed within the ovary this part eventually becomes the seed.

Peat: Partially decomposed plant material that is found where ancient bogs or marshes were located.

Peduncle: The stem of a flower or flower cluster.

Perfect flower: A flower in which both sexes are represented.

Perianth: A descriptive term that includes both calyx and corolla.

Petal: One of the segments forming the corolla; usually the colorful part of a flower.

Petiole: The stalk of a leaf.

Phloem: The part of the vascular system that transports dissolved food (carbohydrates).

Photoperiodism: The flowering response of some plants to the length of day.

Photosynthesis: The production of sugar (carbohydrate) from water and carbon dioxide in the presence of chlorophyll and light.

Pistil: The female sexual structure in the flower, composed of stigma, style, and ovary.

Pollen: Tiny spores containing the male gamete that are developed in the anther.

Pollination: The movement of pollen from the anther to the stigma of the same flower, other flowers on the same plant, or flowers on other plants of the same type.

Receptacle: The end of the flower stalk (frequently enlarged) that bears the flower parts.

Respiration: A process occurring within all living cells in which food (carbohydrate) is combined with oxygen resulting in release of energy.

Root hair: Tubelike extensions of the epidermal cells of roots through which most water is absorbed. They occur in the area of differentiation (maturation).

Sepal: A segment of the calyx.

Stamen: The male portion (pollen bearing) of the flower, consisting of a filament and anther.

Stigma: The part of the pistil that receives the pollen.

Stomate: A naturally occurring opening into the leaf.

Style: The elongated part of the pistil between stigma and ovary.

Taproot: A large main root from which much smaller branch roots spread laterally.

Thermal periodicity: The flowering response of a plant to the alternation of warm and cool temperatures, such as day and night.

Transpiration: The loss of water from a plant in the form of vapor.

Vascular system: A series of tubes called xylem and phloem that form the water and food conducting system in plants.

Vernalization: The flowering response of some plants to a change in temperature.

Woody: Plants like trees and shrubs that have hard stems which increase in diameter each year.

Xylem: The water-conducting portion of the vascular system.

Zygote: The fertilized egg that will eventually become an embryo in a seed. It is the result of the fusion of the male and female gametes.

2

SEED PROPAGATION

Anyone with some money can buy plants. But part of the fun of horticulture is to start your own plants. The following two chapters explain some of the methods you may use for reproducing plants.

The most frequently used means of producing new plants is by planting seeds. Seed propagation has several advantages over other methods. First, it is by far the most economical. A package of garden flower seeds, which may range in price from 35¢ to $1.50, will contain enough seed to produce 50 to 150 plants. Also, very little personal effort is needed for this production. A seldom-mentioned but important fact about seed propagation is that the seedlings produced are usually free of any diseases the parent plants had. A few diseases are transmitted at a low percentage through the seeds but most are screened out. Because seeds need not be used immediately after harvest, we can save them for months or years and use them at our convenience. They must be properly stored, however. Nature sometimes stores seeds accidentally for years. Lotus seeds deposited in lakes in Manchuria and Japan thousands of years ago were uncovered by construction workers in the 1960s. Some of these seeds were sent to university laboratories where they germinated, grew, and flowered. Seed companies and plant breeders are constantly testing various methods of harvesting and storing to enable them to maintain seeds in top condition for longer periods. While most seeds can be kept for some time, they cannot be held indefinitely and still retain their ability to germinate. Most of our common garden seeds may be stored for about three years.

We don't always use seeds for propagation, however, because they have some disadvantages. Many seeds simply require so long to germinate, or the seedlings grow so slowly, that we find it uneconomical. Many of the woody trees, shrubs, and vines are in this category.

Genetic variation of the seedlings is another problem that may arise from seed propagation. If no outside pollen can blow in or be carried in by insects, duplication of plants through seed propagation is fairly constant. However, with most of the open-pollinated flowers in our gardens this is not true. Seed companies make an effort to ensure that outside pollen will not stray into their seed-producing fields. If you want to produce white-flowered petunias, pollen from one blue-flowered petunia could cause hybrid seed to be produced which might yield some white-flowered petunias but could also produce *many other* colors.

Let us look at the garden flower seed industry. To obtain white petunia seed for packaging and sale, a company would grow white petunias in a field isolated by a mile or more from other petunia plants. During the growing season any other flower colors that might appear in the field would be rogued (plants dug up). Seed collected from the remaining plants would be planted in a similar field the following year. After several years' repetition of this procedure the seeds collected from the petunias could be relied upon to produce uniform, white-flowered petunias. This process is called inbreeding. Frequently after long periods of inbreeding a loss in plant vigor may be detected. It might show up as the production of few or smaller flowers, or perhaps the plants might grow more slowly or become more susceptible to disease.

To be successful a seed company must supply its customers not only with quality seed, but with plants which are new and different. Breeding programs are conducted for this purpose. A plant geneticist working for the company plants in isolated chambers in a greenhouse. He tries to produce a new type of flower by making specific crosses of pollen to stigma on separate plants. Let us suppose that he has a short white petunia and a tall red petunia that have developed as a result of inbreeding. One of the crosses he tries in the greenhouse involves pollinating the white petunia flower with pollen collected from the red plant. He must remove the anthers from the white petunia to ensure that no white pollen accidentally is involved. Eventually he collects the seed formed as a result of fertilization in the white petunia, plants it, and discovers his new plant is pink and has a cascading form instead of being either short or tall. Every time he makes the cross the resulting seedlings are pink cascades. He may also find that the new plants are more vigorous than either of the parents. They may produce more and larger flowers, be more disease resistant, and grow faster. These plants are the F_1 generation, the result of planting **hybrid** seeds. The term hybrid simply tells us that two different varieties, or cultivars, were involved in the seed production.

If this new plant is satisfactory, the company will begin to produce enough seeds for commercial sale. The anthers must be removed from a large group of white petunia flowers and all the plants grown in isolation. Pollen is collected (either by hand or by machine) from the red petunia field, carried to the new production area, and dusted on the emasculated white petunias. Eventually the seed from these white petunias is collected and packaged for sale as an exciting new hybrid petunia. The seed will be more expensive than the old inbred seed because of the cost of labor and research involved in its production.

Suppose you plant this new seed and are pleased with the magnificient display; you decide you want the same plants next year but hate to spend the money for those more valuable hybrids. There are no other petunias in the neighborhood—no chance for accidental pollen to disrupt the reproduction of pink cascades. So you collect the seeds that form and plant them next spring. Will you be happy? Probably not. That second year will produce the F_2 generation. All the genes that were involved in the F_1 generation will be scrambled anew and may produce red short, white tall, pink short and tall, white short and cascade, and so on. There may also be a few pink cascades.

While seeds range in size from the large coconut to the dustlike petunia seeds, they all have the same basic structure: seed coat, embryo, and some stored food. The tiny embryo, the result of fertilization, is made up of a **radicle** (primary root), **hypocotyl, cotyledon(s)**, and **epicotyl**. The cotyledons, or seed leaves, are attached at the juncture of hypocotyl and epicotyl. The epicotyl eventually develops into the stem of the plant.

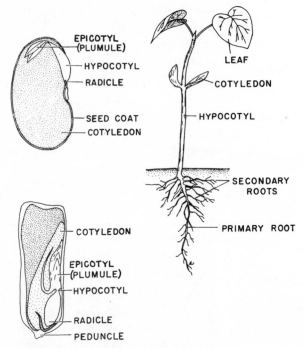

Seed and seedling anatomy

Our interest is not so much in the anatomy as in the germination of the seed. That process begins with the seed absorbing water. This enables enzymes in the seed to convert stored food into sugar—the same sugar produced in the leaves during photosynthesis. It has been transported through the phloem tissues to the seed and converted there into more stable substances such as starch or oil. Now the stored food is transformed back into sugar to become a building block and a source of energy. Oxygen must also penetrate the seed coat to combine with the sugar to release energy (respiration) for the work of building new cells and expanding others. The embryo then begins to expand and soon bursts through the water-softened seed coat. The first portion to emerge is usually the radicle, which we now call the primary root. Eventually the hypocotyl also emerges and in most cases pushes up above ground and the cotyledons expand. Even though the cotyledons are green and look like leaves, they usually are not capable of photosynthesis. They do, however, contain some of the stored food that was originally in the seed, so they furnish sugar for continued growth of the embryo— now called a **seedling**. The epicotyl continues to expand and finally produces a real leaf. While the cotyledons have smooth margins and are rather thick, the true leaves generally are quite different in appearance and are distinctive for each type of plant. Now germination is complete. Because the young seedling has a leaf capable of photosynthesis, it is no longer dependent on the stored food originally contained in the seed.

Thousands of seeds may be produced by a plant each year, but only a few germinate and survive. Many are eaten by birds or are destroyed by insects or soil microorganisms. Many fall in locations unfavorable for germination. For germination to proceed, water, oxygen, and warm temperatures must be present. Water is necessary for enzymatic activity. Oxygen is needed within the seed for respiration. Both must enter through the seed coat. The proper temperature is that at which the optimum rate of biochemical activity will occur. This is the temperature that will produce new tissues fastest. For most garden flower seeds a temperature range of 60° to 80° F. is adequate. Many seeds will germinate satisfactorily in the range 50° to 85° F.

Most seeds germinate more rapidly if they receive some light. This means that seeds buried too deeply simply will not germinate because light cannot reach them. Eventually we may find that light speeds germination of all seeds *if* we have the other environmental factors correctly regulated. But at present there appear to be some seeds whose germination is inhibited by light. Cyclamen seeds, for example, will germinate several weeks sooner in the dark than in the light. The package in which they are sold will indicate this.

A review of the conditions necessary for germination will give you an idea of the proper storage conditions for most seeds. A dry storage at temperatures slightly above freezing should do. Many seeds can even be frozen safely. Ideally we would also control the composition of the atmosphere in the storage area, but that requires expensive equipment and is not normally done.

Seeds which fall to the ground in late summer and have ideal environmental conditions but do not germinate are said to be **dormant**. Dormancy may be physical or physiological. Physical dormancy simply means the seed coat is too hard and tough for water to penetrate. In nature such seeds lie in the soil during the winter while microorganisms attack the seed coat or water freezes around the seed (and thaws and freezes again). By spring the seed coat has been weakened enough so water can penetrate.

Physiological dormancy is more complex. For our purposes we can say that some chemical is present in the seed which inhibits germination, or some chemical necessary for germination is missing. A seed lying in the soil over the winter is soaked repeatedly, and this soaking in water may build the necessary chemical or remove an inhibiting one.

Physical dormancy may be broken by simply cutting the seed coat or soaking the seed for a short time in boiling water or sulfuric acid. We call that **scarification**. Physiological dormancy is broken by **stratification**. This process involves placing seeds in moist peat or sphagnum or sand and storing them at cold temperatures for days, weeks, or months, depending on the particular seed. In most cases the seed-packaging company has broken the dormancy before you buy the seed. In some cases simple directions are included telling you to soak or chill the seed before planting.

Dormancy apparently is a biological mechanism that prevents premature germination when approaching environmental conditions may not be right for seedling growth. These mechanisms seem to disappear in plants which have been extensively bred or hybridized; but weeds and many woody plants still retain them.

Although many seeds can be planted directly in the garden, by the time soil temperatures warm up in the spring it is too late to grow many annuals. Some flowering annuals like sweet alyssum will germinate in cold soil and the plants can stand light frost. Most cannot. Later we will discuss starting seeds directly in the garden. But most garden flower seeds should be germinated indoors, grown until the plants are ready to flower, and then planted outdoors. This means that you should count back six to eight weeks from the earliest frost-free time for planting in your area, and plant the seeds indoors.

If you want to plant seeds economically, use containers found in your kitchen: plastic refrigerator dishes, margarine cups, cottage cheese cartons, milk cartons, casserole dishes, bowls, or pans. My choice would be a container with holes punched in the bottom for drainage. Of course, you can buy plastic, fiber, or wood trays at the garden stores.

Rooting medium: soil

The medium in which you will plant the seeds needs to be considered more carefully. Since moisture and oxygen are both necessary for seed germination, and because many seeds are extremely small, the medium must have quite small particles in order to maintain contact with the seeds. Soil is a poor medium because it does not have enough air or oxygen in it. **Sphagnum moss** which has been screened or milled so the particle size is quite small is an excellent material. These moss plants grow around bogs and marshes in temperate climates. The soil in which they grow is quite acid so not many weeds or disease-causing microorganisms are present. The plants themselves are also quite acid. Each plant contains myriads of large

Rooting medium: sphagnum moss (milled)

cells which can absorb water to the extent of ten to twenty times the weight of the plant.

Horticultural **vermiculite** has been used with considerable success, but the particle size is rather large for use with small seeds. Vermiculite is a material originally developed for insulation. Each particle gives the appearance of being several irregularly shaped slabs glued together. Each of these particles holds considerable moisture on its surface.

Of more recent development is the peatlike mixture which is a combination of moss peat and vermiculite. Peat is simply partially decomposed moss. This is combined with an equal volume of vermiculite to form an excellent medium. **Jiffy-Mix** is a commercial product composed of peat and vermiculite plus some fertilizer all milled to small particles and sterilized. It is used by many florists and nurserymen. If you can't find it locally, it is inexpensive to order by mail because of its light weight.

Rooting medium: vermiculite

Rooting medium: peat

Rooting medium: Jiffy-Mix

Fill the container with the growing medium to within one-half inch of the top, then firm and level this planting bed. Now mark off some shallow rows in which to plant the seeds. Indoors seeds need not be planted very deeply. Never plant them deeper than three times their diameter. Usually one diameter's depth is sufficient. When in doubt, plant shallower than you think necessary. Space the seeds one-fourth to one-half inch apart in the rows.

Row planting and careful spacing reduce the chance of disease. Warm, moist conditions are necessary for seed germination, but they also are conditions under which many soil microorganisms flourish. In years past when young seedlings died soon after they emerged from the soil, it was thought they were killed by excess moisture. The disease was named **damping-off**. We know now that fungi in the soil attack and girdle the emerging stems, and as the top of the seedling elongates it becomes top-heavy and the

Seed propagation: milk carton filled with Jiffy-Mix

weakened stem breaks. Keeping the soil surface free of excess moisture might discourage the growth of these microorganisms. Planting the seeds in rows allows more air circulation between plants and over the soil surface. Even though you start with a disease-free medium, these microorganisms may find their way in on dust particles, water, fingers, or labels. Florists and nurserymen try to maintain aseptic conditions to prevent this disease. You should too.

Wetting the seed medium is best accomplished by dunking the container in water. Do not let water enter over the top. Water should enter the *bottom* of the container through the drainage holes. It will move upwards by capillary action until beads of moisture appear on the surface. The medium is then thoroughly wet. Remove the container from the pan of water and allow it to drain.

The seeds need to be identified in some way so that a month after planting you will remember what was planted. If all the seeds are the same, then one label is enough for the entire container. If each row has different seeds, then each must be labeled.

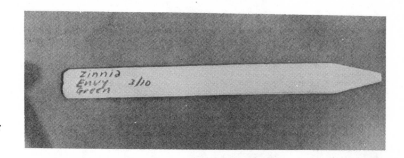

Seed propagation:
preparing a label

To prevent drying of the medium prior to germination, the container should be covered. A clear plastic bag, such as a sandwich bag, will suffice for a small container. Saran wrap, wax paper, or a piece of glass could also be used. When seeds begin to germinate and a few seedlings become visible, the covering should be opened or holes punched in it to let in more air. When most of the seedlings are up, the covering should be removed altogether.

It is not necessary to place seeds in direct sunlight. In fact, that much light will burn the young seedlings. Bright light is sufficient. Many people use a fluorescent light fixture as their light source. This may be placed within six inches of the seedlings without harming them.

After they have developed their first *true* leaves, transplant the seedlings into individual pots. If the plants are being started for the outdoor garden, transplant them into peat pots containing a soil mixture (1 part soil, 1 part peat, 1 part sand). The peat pots are lightweight and have the added advantage of being biodegradable, so they need not be removed when the final planting in the garden is made. Put one plant in each pot. Young seedlings must be handled carefully to prevent breaking the stem. At this tender stage a broken stem means the end of the plant. Following transplanting, the young plants should be given all the sunlight possible.

Seed propagation: cover container with plastic bag

Seed propagation: emerging seedlings showing cotyledons

Seed propagation:
transplanting a seedling

After the seedlings have developed at least three sets of true leaves, those plants you wish to branch should be **pinched**. This means removing the tip of the stem above the third leaf (or third pair of leaves) to allow the axillary buds at the lower nodes to develop into stems. Eventually each of the new branches will bear flowers. Pinching produces a compact plant with heavy foliage and, if it is a flowering plant, lots of flowers. However, if you desire a single tall stem, do not pinch.

One more cultural practice should be discussed here. Taking a plant from a 75° F. room and planting it out in the garden where temperatures at night in the spring may drop to 35° or 40° F. causes growth to stop. The plant has been shocked. It may take several weeks to get it started again. A florists' custom which can alleviate this condition is called **hardening-off**—plants are gradually acclimated to more rigorous environmental conditions. They might be placed outside during the day or left in an unheated sun porch at night. Watering plants less frequently will also slow their growth. Any or all of these things should be done ten to fourteen days before you intend to plant outdoors. This procedure will yield a somewhat tougher plant whose growth, while slowed, continues uninterrupted.

Preplanted gardens of petunias, marigolds, tomatoes, herbs, and other popular plants are available. One such commercial product is called Punch-N-Gro. You don't have to assemble a growing medium, seeds, or container. A few punches with a pencil plus the addition of a prescribed amount of water and your chores are over. Eventually, however, these plants must be transplanted to pots in the manner described.

A seedling growing in a peat pot. Note roots growing through pot.

Seed tapes are available which may be placed directly in the soil. The seeds are spaced at proper distances on the tape, which dissolves when watered. This product saves a little of your own time.

*Pinching—with
knife or fingernails*

*Terminal portion of
stem pinched off*

*Branches resulting
from pinching*

Entire preplanted gardens, an assortment of seeds placed on a type of paper which dissolves after wetting, may also be purchased. These can be unrolled as a border or cut with a scissors to form any desired design. Place the gardens on bare soil, water, and jump back! Of course, you have to accept the manufacturer's choice of plants.

Another commercial innovation named Jiffy-7 is a compressed pot, about the diameter of a silver dollar and one-fourth-inch thick, composed of peat surrounded by a nylon mesh bag. When the disc is placed in water it swells into the shape of a small pot. To use it make a depression in the peat at the open end of the mesh bag, drop in one or two seeds, and that's all. The peat acts as a germinating medium, growing medium, container, and finishing pot. And when planting time comes, you drop pot, plant, and all into the hole you have dug in the garden. Roots grow through the sides of the mesh container.

And more new tricks for easy gardening are on the way!

Jiffy-7's before and after soaking in water

GLOSSARY

Cotyledon: Leaflike structures attached to the embryo, varying in number from one (monocotyledon), to two (dicotyledon), to many.

Damping-off: A disease caused by microorganisms in the soil (pathogenic fungi) that frequently causes death of emerging seedlings.

Dormancy: A condition of inactivity in a seed, bud, or other plant structure. Even though environmental conditions may be correct, no growth occurs.

Epicotyl: The portion of the embryo above the cotyledons including the plumule and the developing stem.

Hardening-off: Process of slowing plant growth gradually through withholding water or reducing temperature prior to outdoor planting to make young plants better able to withstand adverse conditions such as strong winds, cold temperature, and intense sunlight.

Hybrid: A plant resulting from a cross between two parent plants that differ in one or more genes.

Hypocotyl: The portion of the embryo between the radicle (root) and cotyledon.

Jiffy-Mix: A brand name (there are now others) of a commercially prepared mixture of peat and vermiculite plus some minerals.

Pinching: Removing the terminal bud to encourage branching.

Radicle: The lower portion of the embryo that emerges from the seed to become the primary root.

Scarification: A method used to break physical dormancy of seeds through the use of abrasive materials, heat, etc.

Sphagnum moss: A type of plant that grows around bogs and marshes; characterized by having large empty cells (air cells).

Stratification: A method used to break physiological dormancy of seeds by placing them in a moist, low temperature environment.

Vermiculite: An inorganic material used as a rooting medium for propagating plants. It is made from mica subjected to temperatures above 1800° F.

3

ASEXUAL
PLANT PROPAGATION

Years ago people exchanged "slips" to start plants. A slip was usually a piece of stem or a plant leaf used to reproduce the plant from which it was taken. That term is now old-fashioned, but that method of asexual propagation is still very useful and necessary.

Members of the plant world are capable of reproducing themselves from small pieces of root, stem, or leaf. In humans an analogous procedure would be to plant a thumb and grow a new body around it. We take advantage of this reproducing capability to propagate many plants. Seed propagation, as we have seen, is the most economical method, but it is not always possible. To ensure that a new plant is genetically identical to the parent, asexual, or vegetative, propagation is generally used.

The methods of asexual propagation are numerous. We will examine the methods loosely grouped under the terms cutting, bulb, division, offset, runner, layering, and grafting.

A plant like coleus, which can be used as a houseplant or a garden plant, may be started from seed. The seed germinates rather slowly, however, and it takes several months to produce a six-inch-tall plant. But we may plant **cuttings** taken from an existing coleus and produce a six-inch plant in three weeks. This will take a bit more effort and care than seed propagation, and we must start with an existing plant.

Simple stem cuttings are a section of the stem about four to six inches long bearing at least two nodes. The basal end of the cutting is inserted in some rooting medium. With proper care roots will eventually develop somewhere on that stem. We need to determine where roots might form, what type of medium to use, and what environmental conditions would assist the process.

Basically there are three possibilities for root formation, all dependent on meristematic tissue: at the nodes; at the cut end of the stem; adventitiously.

Cuttings: a stem cutting rooting in water

The nodal area is one part of the plant which contains a lot of meristematic tissue. Lateral, or axillary, buds at the nodes may produce roots instead of shoots; however, roots may form anywhere around the stem in the nodal area. If we can provide an environment conducive to root formation, then the nodal area becomes a likely spot for such growth.

The second area of potential root formation is at the cut end of the stem. Meristematic tissue associated with the vascular system probably is involved. In some stems meristematic tissue will cover the wound by forming a **callus**. From the callus roots may emerge, but roots may be produced whether or not a callus forms.

Adventitious roots are those occurring in areas on the stem where we do not anticipate finding them. We cannot predict where they will form. Some plants produce them readily, some not at all.

Unless you have great familiarity with particular plants, you will not know in advance which way roots will be produced. Some plants will produce roots in all three ways, others in only one or two. To make sure roots form, plant stem cuttings in such a way that all three possibilities exist.

The rooting medium is extremely important. It should hold moisture to prevent drying out of the cutting. On the other hand, it should drain freely so that air, and hence oxygen, will be available around the potential root area. This means that the individual particles of the rooting medium should absorb and hold moisture but allow for admission of air between the particles. It should also be disease free, if not sterile. Other desirable qualities would be low cost, light weight, and ready availability.

The most available medium is water. A number of house plants will root in water, although it has been shown that the resulting plants will probably be inferior to those propagated in one of the media described in the following paragraphs. If no better medium is available put aluminum foil over the top of a water filled glass, poke a hole through the foil, and insert stem or leaf cuttings through the hole. Replenish the water as necessary. Roots formed in this manner are apparently not as efficient at extracting moisture from soil as those roots formed in a more solid medium. Eventually the cutting must be transplanted to a solid medium.

An old-time favorite medium was sand. It certainly drains well and is well aerated. It is also cheap and available. However, sand does not retain much moisture, and cuttings dry out quickly even with frequent watering. Sand is not disease free, either, unless heated enough. But it can be used in a pinch if these shortcomings are recognized. It is still used by some florists and nurserymen.

Probably the best material to use is sphagnum moss. These small plants, which grow around bogs and marshes in temperate climates, are harvested, baled, and shipped to the horticulture industry largely from Canada and northern Europe. They may be used in the natural form (sphagnum moss hay) or broken into small pieces called "screened" or "milled" sphagnum. Either form is lightweight, disease free, well aerated, and retains moisture. Moss is rather expensive and not always readily available. It can, however, be purchased by mail, and its light weight means low postage costs for a sizable bag. The moss may be reused, but after a few months' use it begins to decompose.

Another popular material for rooting, vermiculite, is made from mica. Originally developed as an insulating material which you may find in your walls or over the ceiling, smaller pieces have found wide use in horticulture. The particles, formed under intense heat, look like a stack of thin plates, and the irregular surfaces which protrude from this stack hold a considerable quantity of water. The material is sterile, lightweight, and available in lumber yards, garden centers, and grocery stores. Since the particles are relatively large, excess water drains off quickly allowing air to enter the pore spaces. If resterilized, vermiculite may be used over again, but after a few months the plates begin to slip apart, and it is no longer useful.

Perlite is a newer material made by heating lava to an extremely high temperature. The hollow, white particles, somewhat larger than sand grains, permit drainage and yet hold water within themselves. If sterilized by reheating, perlite can be used over and over. Although neither as readily available nor quite as light as the other materials mentioned, it has become the most popular.

Rooting medium: sand

Rooting medium:
sphagnum moss (hay)

Cuttings: plastic bag partially filled with dampened sphagnum moss

Cuttings: producing hole for cutting with a pencil

Rooting medium: perlite

None of these rooting media, however, will provide nutrients necessary for plant growth. Cuttings should be transplanted into a soil mixture as soon as they have at least one root one inch long. Growth will then be almost uninterrupted. Too long a period in the rooting medium will produce roots more subject to damage during transplanting, and the upper part of the cutting will appear pale, washed out, and underdeveloped.

Flowerpots, plastic food containers, cans, milk cartons, bowls, aquariums, or even plastic bags can be used as containers for starting cuttings. It is better if the container has drainage holes, but with careful attention to watering that may not be necessary. A simple way to start a few cuttings is to put two inches of moist sphagnum moss in the bottom of a plastic sandwich bag and insert the cuttings in the moss. Then close the bag for five or six days. At the end of that time open the bag for fifteen minutes each day. Within two or three weeks roots will grow out to the

Cuttings: cutting placed in moss

Cuttings: plastic bag closed

plastic. Since moss remains moist for several weeks, no additional watering is necessary.

Cuttings: a stem cutting of Swedish ivy

Perhaps a word about the mechanics of making a cutting should be inserted here. A section of stem four to six inches long which includes at least two nodes should be cut off on a slant. This may allow more callus to form in some instances. It also produces a larger open area at the end of the xylem tubes through which water can enter. Remove any flowers or flower buds because they use sugar which should be diverted to root production. Remove the leaves from any nodes (at least one) which will be buried, for they can't photosynthesize underground and will only rot. Years ago florists and nurserymen removed many leaves to prevent wilting. Some leaves were cut in half to reduce the transpiring surface area. We know, however, that this also reduced the sugar production area and actually slowed rooting, so we try to reduce transpiration by other methods now. Finally, drill a hole in the rooting medium with a pencil or your finger, drop the cutting in deep enough so it won't tip over, firm the medium around the cutting, and wet the medium.

Now comes the difficult part of starting cuttings. There must be enough moisture to prevent wilting but not enough to permit rotting. A very fine line divides the two. During the first week the problem is primarily wilting. The leaves on the cutting will be losing water (transpiration), and the cutting has only a small area for water intake. The forces which reduce transpiration are high humidity, low light intensity, low temperature, and wilting. Obviously wilting is critical because any growth stoppage now is fatal. Low temperature might help reduce transpiration, but it would also slow the chemical activity necessary to build new root tissue. Light and humidity are the variables to control. Do not put the cuttings in direct sunlight or even extremely bright light until after roots have formed. Try to raise the relative humidity around the cuttings. One way to do this is to put a plastic bag around the cuttings *and* their container; or plant directly in a plastic bag as described earlier. Another technique is to use a double pot. Fill a large pot with perlite or vermiculite (or sand) and insert a small clay pot, with its drainage hole plugged, in the center. Since clay is porous, moisture will seep through the clay into the surrounding medium so long as the center pot is kept filled with water. This provides a constant water supply for the cuttings. The water in the center pot is also constantly evaporating which creates a more humid atmosphere around the leaves of the cuttings.

Cuttings: a stem cutting of Swedish ivy with leaves removed from lower node

Cuttings: double-pot technique showing cork placed in drainage hole of small clay pot

Cuttings: double-pot ready to receive cuttings

Cuttings: stem cuttings placed in perlite

Professional plant propagators use a mist system, a series of nozzles connected to an overhead water pipe. A timing device turns the water on for so many seconds out of a selected time interval (30 minutes, 15 minutes, etc.), sending a very fine spray or mist over the plants. Such a system cools the plants in addition to providing moisture, so the cuttings can be grown in full sunlight. Small versions of mist systems are available for the home owner.

If the cuttings have been covered with plastic in the beginning, they need to be uncovered for a few minutes each day after the first week. Succulent plants, geraniums, and some others may rot if covered at all or even kept very moist. Experience is the biggest help in determining the best conditions for rooting each type of plant.

A kitchen fork may be used to lift cuttings gently after two to three weeks of rooting. If a cutting has roots it should be transplanted into a pot filled with a soil mixture. If roots are not present or are just starting, the cutting can be replaced in its original spot and rechecked the next week.

So far only stem cuttings have been discussed. These may be taken at the tip of a stem, but many cuttings can be made from a single stem if the stem is long enough to meet the criteria for cuttings previously described. Patience plant, chrysanthemum, English ivy, Christmas cactus, wandering Jew, philodendron, aluminum plant, coleus, geranium, and many others may be propagated in this way. Two other types of stem cuttings, which have less use, may also be of interest. A "stem eye" is one in which the stem is cut up into one-node pieces about one and one-half or two inches long. These pieces, with or without leaves, are buried shallowly in a horizontal position. This system is most frequently used when propagating thick-stemmed plants like ti, dracaenas, dieffenbachias, monsteras, and Chinese evergreens, but it may also be used for devil's ivy and geranium. Generally speaking this is a long, slow method, and the original plants are virtually destroyed, so it is usually a desperation method.

Cuttings: stem eye cuttings of dieffenbachia rooted and unrooted

Another type of stem cutting is misnamed "leaf eye" (leaf bud) cutting. A leaf is removed with its petiole and also a sliver of stem including the axillary bud. The wound on the stem will heal eventually. The cutting will root slowly. Hydrangeas generally are propagated this way; geraniums may be also, but geraniums root so much faster from stem tip cuttings that leaf buds are seldom used.

Cuttings: leaf bud cutting of geranium

Cuttings: leaf bud cutting placed in perlite

One other type of cutting is a leaf cutting. Watermelon plant and African violet may be propagated by removing a leaf with one to two inches of petiole. The petiole is inserted to a depth that brings the leaf blade in contact with the rooting medium. Succulent-leaved plants also can be rooted this way. If no petiole exists, insert the leaf blade deep enough to prevent the cutting from tipping.

Cuttings: a leaf cutting rooting in water

Sansevierias (mother-in-law's tongue and others) may be propagated by cutting a leaf into four-to six-inch sections and inserting each piece deep enough to stand vertically. Roots will form all along the lower edge, providing that really was the lower part of the leaf section, but it isn't easy to tell which end is up in a leaf section taken from the middle of a sansevieria leaf.

Rex begonias provide an example of one other possible type of leaf cutting. If you have sufficient propagating space, place the entire leaf blade flat on the rooting medium. With part of the petiole acting as an anchor, pin the blade in place or use pebbles or sand scattered on top to keep the leaf in contact with the medium. Then sever each of the main veins in the leaf with a knife or razor. New plants will form at the cuts. There is a modification of this method for use where propagating room is not plentiful. In this case, cut the leaf blade into wedgeshaped sections using the point of attachment of the petiole as the point of the wedge. Then square off the point of each wedge and plant remaining pieces vertically, like a sansevieria leaf section. Each leaf blade section must include a major vein to allow the new plant to start from the cut end of the vein.

Cuttings: leaf cuttings placed in perlite

If you are wondering how to determine which kind of cutting to make, there is a simple rule: If the plant has a stem, use it for a cutting. Obviously, a plant with no visible stem must be propagated by leaf cuttings. Like everything else biological, that rule won't work 100 percent of the time—but probably 90 percent.

*Cuttings: Rex begonia leaf
prior to propagation*

*Cuttings: Rex begonia leaf
cut into wedge-shaped segments*

Cuttings: Rex begonia leaf segment with main vein cut

Cuttings: Rex begonia leaf segment ready for propagation

Cuttings: Rex begonia leaf segment placed in perlite

Nature has provided the means for a number of plants to propagate themselves. Strawberry, airplane plant, and vining violet produce **runners**, which are modified stems. These runners have nodes. Small plants form at some of the nodes and will take root if they are in contact with a moist growing medium. Once roots have formed, the runner, also called a **stolon**, may be severed. The plantlets are genetically identical to the parent.

Another natural method of propagation is with **offsets**, horizontal branches formed at the crown of the plant. The best example of an offset is the succulent plant (actually many different plants) called hen-and-chickens. The parent plant puts out a number of short branches around its base. Each of these branches may root. The overall result is a big plant surrounded by many smaller plants, hence hen-and-chickens. These offsets may be removed and planted individually. Members of the pineapple family, called bromeliads, are also propagated this way. For the screw pine it is the only method of propagation.

Miscellaneous propagation: strawberry showing stolons

An array of underground plant storage structures is grouped under the classification of **bulbs**; however, only a few of them actually are bulbs. A true bulb is a compressed shoot that has leaf and stem tissue. The stem is compressed with modified leaves, called scales, arranged in concentric rings around the growing point (e. g., onions), or randomly (e. g., lilies). Hyacinths, amaryllis, daffodils, and tulips are all true bulbs.

*Miscellaneous propagation:
stolons of airplane (spider) plant*

*Miscellaneous propagation:
offsets formed by hen-and-chickens*

Miscellaneous propagation:
screw pine

Miscellaneous propagation:
bulbs of daffodil, hyacinth, lily

Miscellaneous propagation:
corm and tuberous root

Miscellaneous propagation:
rhizome of iris

The **corm** also is a bulblike structure but has little or no leaf tissue. It is really a compressed stem. When cut open, the corm appears to be solid flesh. Paper material around the outside may be remnants of what once was leaf material but is no longer essential to the growth of the corm. Cyclamen, crocus, and gladiolus are all produced from corms.

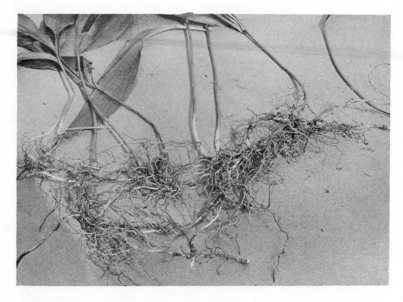

Miscellaneous propagation:
rhizome of lily-of-the-valley

Rhizomes do not look like bulbs but are frequently listed with them in books and catalogs. Rhizomes are underground stems which grow horizontally. They usually are thick and fleshy as with iris and cannas but some, such as lily-of-the-valley and some turf-grasses, are rather slender. These may be dug and stored like bulbs.

Tubers are enlarged, fleshy portions of underground stems, primarily storage organs, that are distinguished from roots by the presence of nodes. The common potato is an example. The eyes of the potato are the nodes. The entire potato could be planted but we usually use pieces containing one or two nodes (eyes).

A **tuberous root** is similar to a tuber but it possesses no nodes. It is root tissue, not stem. These fleshy, swollen roots serve as storage organs. Sweet potatoes, dahlias, peonies, daylilies, and some begonias may be propagated with their tuberous roots.

A number of other asexual means of propagation exist. Some of them are not of much interest to amateur gardeners. One that is of interest and is in common use is **division**. Division is merely dividing up a plant into a series of pieces. A plant like the common garden phlox is planted originally with several stems arising from a small root system. But, after five or six years this same plant may have twenty or more stems and be encroaching on other plants in your garden. In the fall after several hard freezes, simply dig up the root system and cut it with a knife into four or five sections. Each section must have some roots attached to the base of some stems. These are individual "crowns." One of these sections should be replanted in the hole from which you dug the plant. Other sections may be planted elsewhere, given away, or destroyed.

*Division: **African violet removed from pot***

A houseplant such as the African violet may be divided similarly. The leaves will appear to arise from several different places in the pot where the plant has been growing. Before dividing knock the plant out of the pot and observe the formation of multiple crowns

Division: crowns separated and roots cut

Division: knife placed between crowns

along the soil surface. Then cut through the soil ball between the crowns and separate the tangled leaves carefully. Each of these divisions should then be potted in a container equal in size to the one from which it was removed. Any houseplant which forms multiple crowns can be divided, for example, ferns, sansevierias, and cast iron plant.

Layering is a method used commonly in nursery propagation in years past but seldom used today. For the home owner, however, it provides a "last chance" method for reproducing some of the woody shrubs and vines. If other methods fail, try layering. Early in the summer, soon after new growth appears, pull a branch of the shrub you wish to propagate down to the ground, burying the tip and several nodes three or four inches. Anchor the tip in place with a stake so wind movement through the shrub will not disturb it. Several months later, if you are lucky, roots will have formed at or near some of the nodes. The stem tip can then be severed from the branch, and you will have a new plant genetically identical to the parent plant. Actually, you are rooting a cutting without first removing it from the parent plant. Various tricks can speed up the rooting process, such as cutting part way through the buried section or winding a wire around it. Then, too, you may try placing a long section of branch in a trench or weaving it in and out of the soil in serpentine fashion. All of these methods are too slow and space consuming for commercial use.

One type of layering is used commercially, however, and will be of value to the home owner—that is air layering. With this method roots can be produced on stems above the soil. The reasons for doing this may not be readily apparent. Suppose your rubber plant has grown so well it threatens to touch the ceiling. Air layering will enable you to save the top section of the stem and start a new plant. Or, suppose you have a dieffenbachia which has lost many of its lower leaves but continues to grow. Air layering will save the plant and make it more attractive.

Division: crowns pulled apart yielding two plants

The air layering process involves making an up-ward-slanting cut about one third of the way through the stem at a point where you wish a new root system to develop. This point should be high enough so only five or six leaves are above it. (With dicotyledonous plants a ring of bark about one inch wide could be removed from around the stem rather than making a cut. This will produce roots faster but does not work with monocotyledonous plants. The cut into the stem will work with both kinds of plants.) To prevent the cut from closing, insert a match or toothpick into it. Around this area, place a ball of sphagnum moss which has been soaked in water for several hours. Use as much moss as you can hold between your hands. To keep it in place and prevent drying, cover it with Saran wrap or plastic—a split-open sandwich bag will work nicely. Use string or twist ties to hold everything in place. See that the moss does not protrude from the wrapping; moss that is not covered dries rapidly, pulling moisture from the remaining moss. It must remain moist for at least six or eight weeks. Now just wait for roots to grow through the moss to the plastic. By severing some of the phloem, this procedure blocks the downward passage of some of the sugar formed in the leaves. In an environment suitable for root formation, the blocked sugar will be used to build new root tissues. If no roots appear after eight weeks, the process has failed. But just unwrap the stem and the plant will continue growing as before—no harm has been done. In all probability, however, roots will be visible after four weeks. Allow another four to six weeks for enough root development to handle the water supply needed for the remaining leaves on the plant. Then unwrap the plastic and cut the stem off just below the sphagnum ball, which should remain intact. Place this new, shorter plant in a pot about the same size as that in which the plant previously grew. Take care to prevent high rates of transpiration for several weeks until more extensive root growth has occurred.

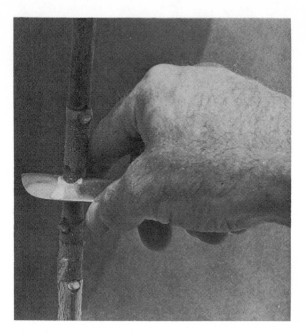

Air layering: make an upward, slanting cut about ⅓ through the stem

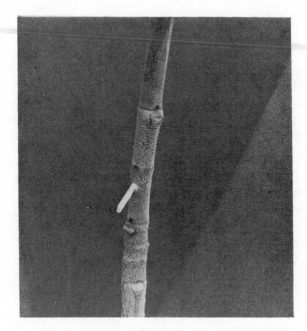

Air layering: hold the wound open by inserting a matchstick in it

Air layering: wrap a handful of moist sphagnum moss around the cut

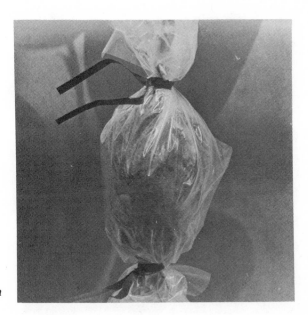

Air layering: cover the moss with clear plastic and fasten it in place

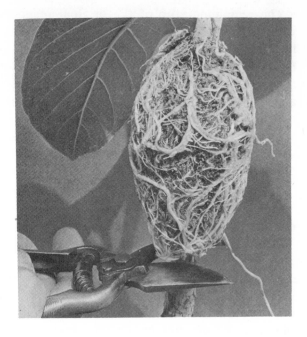

Air layering: remove plastic, sever stem beneath moss

Air layering: place new root system in pot and cover with soil

The remaining stub of the original plant might as well be dumped. Occasionally one or two of the lateral buds will start to grow; usually they do not. Even if they do grow, the resulting branches jut out to the sides and the plant takes on a short, wide appearance rather than a tall, slender look. In a greenhouse, where light and humidity are plentiful, lateral buds do grow, and the side branches they produce are themselves air layered yielding an increase in plant numbers. The same general system is used in Florida in the propagation of some of the tall houseplants.

The last method of asexual propagation we shall consider is **grafting**. The home owner will have only a limited opportunity to employ grafting, but nurserymen use it to produce fruit trees, roses, and many ornamental trees and shrubs. Basically, grafting involves uniting two separate plants. One of the plants must provide the root system while the other provides the desired fruit, foliage, or flowers.

Two stories will illustrate why grafting might be necessary. When the grape industry was first established in California in the nineteenth century, European grape varieties were used. Many years later for some mysterious reason plants began to die in large numbers. Eventually it was discovered that a soil insect was destroying the roots of these imported European grapes. Meanwhile, native American grapes were seemingly untroubled by the insect. Unfortunately, however, the native plants did not produce grapes which could be eaten or made into wine. Certainly they were not comparable to the European varieties. The problem was to produce a grape plant with American roots and European grapes. This was done, and the California grape industry was saved. The method used was grafting.

A second story concerns roses. Garden roses need a hardy root system that spreads down and out to extract moisture from a large soil area. But many roses are grown in greenhouses around the country where their flowers are cut for year-round commercial sale. Hardiness is not necessary and an extensive, deep root system is not possible. In a greenhouse bench in which roses are grown the soil is only eight to ten inches deep and plants are grown close together for economy. They need a special root system of many fibrous, shallow roots. A rose having such a root system is selected to serve as a rootstock for a greenhouse rose. The desired flowering plant is then grafted to that root system.

Grafting, then, consists of an **understock** (root system) and **scion** (variety of desired stem). The scion is cut in the same manner as a stem cutting. The plant being used for the understock has its top removed by a slanting cut. The two pieces then are drawn together so their meristematic tissues will be in contact over the greatest possible distance; meristematic area in these woody plants is a thin layer directly under the bark. This joint is then wrapped with tape or wound with rubber to keep it from slipping until healing occurs. The meristematic tissues eventually form new xylem and phloem bridging the joined areas. Modifications of this system are frequently used that add strength to the union. The length of the scion will vary from a single node piece about one and one-half inches long (some greenhouse roses) to twelve-inch sections of stem possessing numerous nodes (apples and others).

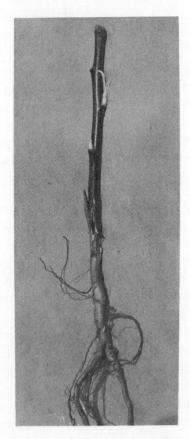

Miscellaneous propagation: freshly grafted apple tree

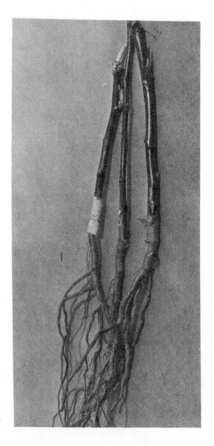

Miscellaneous propagation: graft unions wrapped

A variation of grafting known as bud grafting, or, more frequently, just **budding**, is more common in nursery propagation than the standard method previous described. In budding, a single bud is used for the scion instead of a piece of stem. This is an economy of material, and the method is highly successful. A rootstock or understock is still used, but it must be growing and not dormant as may be the case in standard grafting. A T-shaped cut is made through the bark near the soil surface and the bark pulled back from the T to permit insertion of the scion bud. This scion bud, cut from the side of a stem, consists of a thin piece of bark, including the leaf and lateral bud, measuring one-half to one inch in length. The leaf is removed but a bit of the petiole remains as a "handle." The scion bud is then slipped into the slot in the bark. After insertion of the bud, the bark is replaced as nearly as possible in its original position and a flat piece of rubber is wrapped carefully but snugly around this union. Once the bud begins to grow, the top part of the understock plant is cut off immediately above the union. If the bud doesn't grow, another attempt can be made on the same understock. The resulting new plant has a right-angle jog at its base, but as it grows this becomes less and less noticeable.

Miscellaneous propagation:
bud-grafted rose

By grafting scions onto certain understocks it is possible to produce trees and shrubs of smaller than normal size. With apples, for example, a specific understock, a crab apple called East Malling IX (E. M. IX), will prevent the normal elongation of the stem and branches of any apply variety grafted onto it. The resulting tree will be about half normal size, but the fruits will be full size. Other specific understocks will produce a range of tree sizes somewhere between this dwarf and full size. Modern orchards are planted with these dwarfed apple trees because yield per acre is increased. Besides saving space because they can be planted closer together, these trees are more easily sprayed, pruned, and picked. Other fruit trees like plums, cherries, peaches, and pears can also be reduced in size by grafting them on dwarfing understocks. Grafting by itself will not reduce size. Only those specific dwarfing understocks, discovered by accident or research, will cause size reduction.

Perhaps it should be pointed out that with a few exceptions the scion and understock must be closely related plants or the union between them will not heal. Roses are grafted to roses. Apples are grafted on apples—although they may be crab apples.

It has been found that a section of stem taken from a dwarfing apple understock and used as an interstem between the desired scion and a nondwarfing understock will also produce a dwarfing effect. The amount of dwarfing may not be quite as great as if the entire root system were used. The reason for using an interstem system is to employ more vigorous understock but still produce the dwarfing effect. So now we may have a crabapple understock, to which is grafted a dwarfing interstem, to which is grafted a variety of apple like Red Delicious. These three plants united produce an apple tree that will grow vigorously, produce many top quality apples, but remain a small tree. The process may be taken a step further. As a home owner you may wish to have more than one kind of apple but have room for only one tree. With this three-part tree we have started, we can graft (bud graft) four or five other varieties onto the original Red Delicious. These will all produce normal apples. Such a tree can be purchased from a number of nurseries.

Grafting has been known and used for more than two thousand years. We are still learning new ways of using it. In fact, the entire field of plant propagation is being changed and added to nearly every day. It is a fascinating subject.

GLOSSARY

Adventitious: Plant structures such as shoots or roots produced in unexpected areas on the plant.

Budding: A type of grafting in which a single bud becomes the scion.

Bulb: An underground structure produced naturally by some plants; essentially a compressed shoot (leaf and stem). It may be used to propagate plants.

Callus: Tissue produced by a plant to cover a wound.

Corm: An underground structure much like a bulb but containing only stem tissue.

Cuttings: Pieces of plant stem, leaf, or root used to propagate new plants.

Division: A method of propagating some plants by separating the crowns.

Grafting: A method for plant propagation that involves uniting the stem (scion) of one plant to the root system (understock) of another closely related plant.

Layering: A method of propagation that forces roots to be produced on stems that are still attached to the parent plant.

Offsets: Short branches produced at the crown of the plant that look like the parent. They may be broken off and rooted much like cuttings. Frequently they produce roots while still attached.

Perlite: An inorganic material used for plant propagation. It is produced by heating volcanic lava to a temperature of around 2200° F.

Rhizome: An underground stem, usually thickened, that grows horizontally.

Runner: See Stolon.

Scion: A portion of the stem or a bud used in grafting. The scion is the desired above ground portion of the grafted combination.

Stolon: (Also called a runner) Similar to a thin rhizome but growing above ground. Roots and shoots may form at the nodes.

Tuber: A naturally occurring underground storage structure similar to a corm but thicker and having "eyes" (nodes), e. g., the common potato.

Tuberous root: Similar to a tuber but made up of root tissue with no "eyes" (nodes), e. g., the sweet potato.

Understock: The lower portion of a grafted plant that includes the roots.

*

4

HOUSEPLANTS

Flower and vegetable growing outdoors seems to be an interest kindled early in life. Many people are outdoor gardeners. However, not as many people are aware of the joys of indoor gardening, and in half of our country the indoor season is longer.

Before turning to the special requirements of specific houseplants, it will be useful to go over some general information about growing plants indoors.

The plants we call houseplants generally will stand the heat and lack of humidity in our homes as well as the limited amount of light. (Many plants are sold as houseplants even though they cannot endure one of those environmental conditions. Such plants should not be used.) If we understand how to manipulate the environment, we may do a better job raising houseplants.

Light is necessary for photosynthesis. But plants have different light requirements. For some a low level of light intensity will be enough to sustain adequate photosynthesis. For other plants that light intensity may not even start photosynthesis. Obviously photosynthesis must exceed respiration or the plant will lose ground. Photosynthesis at a low rate may not produce enough sugar to exceed that used in respiration under the existing day length. But suppose you extend the day length with artificial lighting. Then the total amount of sugar produced might exceed that used in respiration even though the light intensity is lower than usually required. This is one of the tricks used to supplement photosynthetic activity. Of course, the obvious thing would be to increase light intensity. This could be done by adding artificial lights or placing the plant near a window or a brighter window.

A measure of light intensity is the **footcandle**. In theory one footcandle is the light intensity found at the distance of one foot in any direction from a lighted candle. This unit of measure is not highly regarded in scientific research anymore but will serve our purpose. You can read with 25 footcandles of light. Studying or sewing would be better done at 50 footcandles. At 500 footcandles the shadow of your hand will be rather sharply outlined against a plant if your hand is passed between the light source and the plant.

The *kind* of light isn't terribly important. The old incandescent bulbs produce a lot of heat and cannot, therefore, be placed close to foliage, but they do provide high light intensities. They also produce a preponderance of wave lengths near the red end of the spectrum, the area that stimulates photosynthesis most. Fluorescent lamps illuminate without giving off much heat and can be brought to within a few inches of foliage. They produce more light in the blue end of the spectrum, and plants grow more compactly. A combination of incandescent and fluorescent light is probably best if sunlight never enters the room. Sunlight however, provides the full spectrum.

Small leaves, longer-than-normal internodes, yellowing, and dropping of leaves are all signs of insufficient light. These symptoms may take several months to develop. Without a normal plant available for comparison, dwindling leaf size, especially, is a difficult symptom to discern.

The yellowing of leaves owing to insufficient light is called **etiolation**. Extreme cases occur during bulb forcing. The shoots emerge above the soil of the pot in a dark refrigerator or a pit in the ground. When they are taken into the light for quick development of flowers, the shoots are white or yellow. Chlorophyll soon begins to develop, and the plant becomes green. Conversely, a plant taken from the light and put in a dark room for several days will begin to lose its green color.

Phototropism is a plant response to light: the leaves or stem bend toward a light source. Some plants respond quickly. Leaves on a few trees will actually turn during the day so that the leaf blades are at right angles to the sun. Most houseplants respond more slowly, but in a week or two their leaves will be turned toward the light source. This reaction suggests that light is not evenly distributed but comes through a single window or from one bright lamp. Stems of plants also will bend toward the light. Plants with woody stems soon stiffen in this bent position and cannot be straightened. To prevent leaf turning or stem bending, turn houseplants ninety to a hundred and eighty degrees each week.

You can use phototropism to advantage. If you know that company is coming in a few weeks, let the leaves turn toward the light. You will be looking at the pale undersides of the leaves during this time. But on the evening you entertain, turn the plants around toward the room; they will appear much fuller and more attractive—but only from one side. Only you need to know it is an illusion. Similarly, some plants with woody stems can be made to assume grotesque shapes by purposely allowing the stems to bend permanently.

The last of the light-related phenomena that should be mentioned is the one called photoperiodism. This term refers to the flowering response of a plant to the length of day and was discussed earlier in the section on flower bud initiation.

The most important point of this section on light is that you must select plants that will live under the light intensities you can readily provide. Do not try to grow geraniums in a room with only a north window. Pick a plant which will endure low light intensities (some are presented in the following chapter).

Having selected the correct houseplant for the available light, why might you have difficulty growing it? Application of water! Watering is probably the most difficult of plant care duties. Two identical plants in the same room will look entirely different in six months with different persons watering them. Watering frequency is largely a matter of judgment. If a plant wilts, obviously it was not watered soon enough. Unfortunately, no such immediate sign is evident if you water too frequently. Eventually weak growth, light green or yellow leaves, even leaf drop will indicate that roots have been damaged by overwatering. My guess is that more plants are damaged by overwatering than underwatering.

Perhaps a review of the factors affecting water use by the plant will be of some help. First of all, the conditions that increase transpiration are going to increase the water consumption of any plant. Temperature, humidity, light, and ventilation have all been discussed earlier. A plant in flower will use more water than one not in flower. Water storage capability of the soil in which a plant is growing will be affected by the soil structure. If you have made up your own soil mixture, you will know its capability, but otherwise that is almost impossible for you to determine. The size of the plant will matter, and the size of the pot will, too. A large plant will use more water than a small one. A large pot will have more water storage capacity than a small pot, so it will need less frequent watering. The type of container also makes a big difference. For example, a clay pot is porous. Water will be lost right through its sides. A plastic, metal, or glazed container will not allow the soil to dry out so rapidly. That might sound good, but the problem here is that the surface soil may *look* dry while moisture is plentiful farther down in the pot. With a clay container, when the surface soil looks and feels dry, chances are the entire soil ball around the roots is also dry. Drainage holes in the bottom of a plant container will allow excess water (the amount beyond the soil's capacity for storage) to escape. Containers without drainage holes may look dry on the surface but have water at the bottom that prevents air from entering the pore spaces and ultimately stops root growth. Roots may even rot.

Generally, we can say: Water a plant when the surface soil is dry enough to crumble between your fingers, but keep these other factors in mind. In any case, water before the plant wilts, for a wilting plant stops growing. Photosynthesis stops but respiration continues. Reserve sugars are used up. Leaves may fall, further reducing sugar production potential. This is a severe setback to the plant.

There are three basic methods for watering houseplants. The first is the simplest and most used. Pour water on the soil surface until the space between the soil and the top of the pot is full. Wait until the water disappears. If no water comes out of the drainage hole, fill that space with water again. Repeat this at five minute intervals until water finally runs out from the bottom of the pot. This means the soil has absorbed all it can hold, but excess water has drained off allowing air to enter the soil. If the container has no drainage hole, you can only water by guess. I would suggest you use a container with drainage holes. Failing that, one possible method is to insert a funnel several inches into the soil and fill it until the water stops running out. Then, place your finger in the throat of the funnel and pull it out of the soil. This method is only slightly better than watering by guess.

A second method also requires a drainage hole in the container. Instead of applying water to the surface, place the base of the container in a pan of water. The water level in the pan must be *below* the top of the container. Water will enter through the bottom and by capillary action move to the surface. When water droplets appear on the surface of the soil, remove the container from the pan of water and allow it to drain. The soil will have been filled to capacity.

A third method, **wick watering**, involves planting in specially constructed containers with a built-in water reservoir. The water does not touch the soil but is transmitted to it by a wick or sponge or both. Recently variations of this method utilizing hollow-walled containers have been introduced. All of these are fine for people who are away from home for days at a time or who habitually forget to water plants. But with the exception of African violets, few of the common houseplants will thrive with this watering system; they simply never get thoroughly watered. They will remain alive, however, and will not wilt. For many people these containers provide the only practical watering method.

In areas of the country where "hard" water prevails (most of the Midwest) the dunking, or immersion, method has one disadvantage. As water evaporates from the soil, the salts (which make water hard) are left in the soil. Eventually, the accumulation of these salts will create a condition which prevents water from entering the plant. Water may even be extracted from the plant. This may cause tips or margins of leaves to turn brown, yellowing of foliage, weak growth, or wilting. All of these symptoms indicate damage to the root system. The same thing may happen with top watering if there is no drainage hole in the container. On the other hand, with drainage provided, top watering leaches the soil of old salts. There is no accumulation of salts, because the water is applied in such volume that excess water drains out carrying with it some of the salts deposited by the previous watering.

Most plants cannot tolerate having their roots sitting in water. Overwatering leads to an accumulation of water in the pore spaces. This prevents oxygen from reaching the roots and stops respiration, and hence growth. So do not let the roots sit in water! Also, try not to wet the foilage when watering, for disease frequently starts on wet foliage. Some plant leaves will show discolored areas where water sits on them. Finally, the temperature of the water should be the same as that of the room in which the plant is growing. If cold water is drawn from the faucet in the winter and dumped on the soil, the soil temperature will be drastically lowered and root growth will stop. When roots stop growing, the plant stops growing. Allow the water to warm up, or mix hot and cold until it feels near room temperature.

When we talk about overwatering or underwatering a plant, we are describing the *frequency* of watering—not the amount of water applied. A plant that requires a lot of water can only be watered with a certain volume because the rest will drain out of the pot. But it can be watered a day or two later with an equal volume. A plant requiring very little water will be watered thoroughly as described previously, but a long interval (a week or ten days) must be allowed before the next watering. Most damaging is to give the plant a little water every day.

Ventilation is not an important factor in houseplant care. Plants, like people, prefer moderate temperatures and moderate air circulation. Excessive drafts simply increase transpiration. Some plants (like the rubber plant) drop their leaves if grown in a drafty spot. Ventilation and watering do influence the relative humidity around plants, and that is important!

Many plants which we grow as houseplants came originally from the jungle. They thrive on rather high relative humidity. Cacti and other succulent plants are exceptions which grow better with low, rather than high, relative humidity. Humidifiers placed in rooms or attached to the furnace will help raise the humidity during the winter when the usual household humidity approaches that of a desert. Another method of maintaining humidity is to group houseplants close together. As they transpire, the relative humidity in the area around the plants is increased. Placing plants on gravel in a metal tray to which water is regularly added will also help. The water is constantly evaporating from the surface and adding moisture to the air. The water level must be below the bottom of the pots, however, or root rotting may occur. Least effective, but better than doing nothing, is to apply a fine mist from a spray bottle over and around the plants several times each day. This provides a temporary increase in relative humidity.

Houseplants have become houseplants because they can endure the temperatures we maintain in our homes. A few will grow better in rooms where temperatures are low (50° to 60° F.). Some will flower more where temperatures vary from day to night. All will resent being kept close to a window on –20° nights. In fact, whenever night temperatures go below freezing, the room temperature close to a window will be too cold for houseplants. Just like using cold water, cold air temperature will chill the soil and the roots. Growth stops. The type of window–storm window combination you have will, of course, be an influence. But to be on the safe side on cold nights, either move the plants away from the window or put magazines or newspapers between them and the glass for insulation.

Plants which grow in pots need nutrients just as garden plants do. The pots limit the amount of soil from which nutrients may be extracted by the plants, so it becomes necessary to add fertilizer. Unfortunately, many people overfertilize houseplants. If there is plenty of light and water, plants will grow and use nutrients. If light is limited, adding fertilizer will *not* increase growth; the fertilizer will be unused. It will accumulate in the soil, and if enough accumulates, it will act like the previously described hard-water salts. Water will be unable to enter the plant and may even be extracted. The plant will die.

Foliage plants are usually grown under low light conditions. Even when light is plentiful, we really do not want foliage plants to grow too rapidly because they soon outgrow the container and the location in the home for which they were bought. For both reasons fertilizing foliage plants should be restricted to three times each year. Between November and March there just is not enough light available for rapid plant growth. I would recommend fertilizing in March, again in May, and again in September.

Flowering plants will need a bit more fertilizer because nutrients are used and lost in the flower-building process, and flowering plants must be given more light. My suggestion is to fertilize them every six or eight weeks until mid-November and resume that process about mid-February.

Fertilizer is available in powder or liquid form. The powders are cheaper but do require your time to dissolve them in water. Directions on the packages will probably suggest using fertilizer more frequently than I have recommended. There are also some slow release fertilizers, granules about the size of BBs, that release nutrients on the soil surface whenever the plant is watered. Since only small amounts are released at a time, a handful might take four to six months to become exhausted. Plant tablets which act much the same way are also available. Wooden sticks that look like tongue depressors or ice-cream bar sticks and are coated with fertilizer are also on the market. This fertilizer, too, is released a little at a time as water is added. Perhaps I am overly cautious about fertilizing, but most damage to houseplants is caused by overwatering and overfertilizing.

Plants get dusty. Like the furniture in your rooms they will have be dusted or cleaned. Such cleaning must be done for a more basic reason than just cleanliness. Dust on the leaf surface reduces the amount of light reaching the chloroplasts. If the dirt layer interferes with photosynthesis too much, the plant will lose more sugar through respiration than it can produce with a reduced rate of photosynthesis. The plant may die. Dust can be removed easily and inexpensively by placing the plant in the sink, covering the top of the soil and pot with aluminum foil, and using the spray attachment to wash off the foliage. You must be sure the soil is carefully covered. Slit the aluminum foil so that it fits snugly around the stem. Failure to do a good job here will result in a disaster to the sink. If no spray attachment is available, wipe the leaves with a cloth using mild soap and water. Again, the soil must be covered to prevent soapy water from damaging the roots. A big plant may be cleaned by carefully covering the soil and placing the plant in the shower.

Various plant-cleaning materials can be purchased. If you do not mind spending some money, the aerosol leaf polishes sold under a variety of names are a convenient item. Just a fast spraying over the foliage will shine the leaves rapidly and produce a hard, bright shine, and the leaves seem to stay clean for quite a while. These sprays are not effective on leaves which have many surface hairs like African violets. But I do not know any plants that they might harm. If you have a lot of plants and need to clean them in a hurry, the aerosol sprays are your best bet.

Milk has been recommended for years as a material for cleaning plant leaves. You may wipe the leaves with milk to clean them if you wish. It will not do a better job than any of the methods listed above, nor will it do any harm.

The African violet is a problem plant to clean. Water on the leaves will cause discoloration. Aerosol spray will not clean them. I have tried a soft brush and failed to clean the leaves. A pipe cleaner twisted into a loop was ineffective in removing dust unless I pressed hard—which tore up the leaf surface and destroyed the leaf. About all you can use is warm water from a sprayer; then shake the leaves after washing to remove any standing water. There may still be some leaf discoloration.

Plants can live in your house year after year so long as they have the proper light, temperature, and water. They even enjoy air conditioning in the summer. But plants which have been existing on the borderline with inadequate light can be rejuvenated in the summer. Simply place them outdoors *in the shade.* Shade during the summer will provide more light than you usually can find in the house. Plants transpire more rapidly outdoors because of air movement and warmer temperatures, so you must be careful not to let them get dry. Late in the summer, before you bring them indoors, spray them twice with an insecticide at about a five-day interval. This will help to eliminate any garden pests, which you certainly will not want to support in your living room all winter.

Frequently when you buy a new plant you import insects with it that the florist failed to eliminate. Individual pests may be picked off or touched with a cotton-tipped toothpick dipped in alcohol. But most of the real insect pests are too small and numerous for these methods. Several methods for disinfesting plants are available. One that some florists use is to mix a pail of insecticide (whatever one your garden center or florist recommends), then cover your hands with rubber gloves and dip the foliage in this liquid. Less troublesome and less effective is spraying the insecticide on the foliage. Least troublesome but most expensive is the aerosol spray which contains insecticides (and often fungicides too). This, like the aerosol for cleaning leaves, is the simplest and quickest to use.

One problem the home owner faces occasionally is what to do with houseplants while on a vacation. Ideally, of course, you would like to have someone come in several times each week and care for them. That isn't always possible. Several wick watering systems are available commercially. Most of them require a drainage hole in the container through which water will enter. Some claim to draw water directly from a reservoir into the upper soil area. All of them depend on having an adequate reserve of water. An inexpensive substitute is to place plants in the bathtub with two or three inches of water drawn in the tub. Success here depends on the tightness of the drain stopper, available light, and length of vacation. Another possibility, but a risky one, is to water the plant thoroughly and then drop a plastic bag over it. The bag should be large enough not to touch the leaves, and support must be provided with a stake or yard-stick. The plant must be kept out of direct sunlight. The function of the bag is to reduce transpiration by providing an area of high relative humidity around the plant. The danger is that it might provide too much humidity and cause rotting to begin.

Double-potting is a method that can be used by most home owners to make watering a less risky routine and to extend the time between waterings. Select a container for its beauty or character, without regard to its utilitarian value, and line it with sphagnum moss. The plant you wish to display in the container should be growing in a clay pot. Place the potted plant in the new container, which must be at least two inches wider and deeper than the pot containing the plant, and pack more moss around the sides. Some sphagnum moss can be put over the soil as well. When the double-potting is completed, a casual observer will not know that two pots are involved. The advantage of double-potting is that the inner pot, after watering, will have some of its excess moisture absorbed by the moss. If the soil in the inner pot should dry out, water will move from the moss through the porous sides of the clay pot. The sphagnum moss becomes a sort of safety valve to protect the plant from either under- or overwatering. In addition, the room decor is improved by the visible container while the plant continues to thrive in a clay pot. Double-potting may also serve as a type of vacation care if both soil and sphagnum moss are watered heavily. Under most conditions the plants will hold for seven to ten days.

Almost everyone who grows houseplants has a problem with a plant eventually. While it is very difficult to analyze such problems from a distance, a few of the symptoms and their possible causes are described here to assist you.

If the leaves of your plants begin to appear yellow or light green and some of the lower leaves drop off, you should suspect root damage. Over- or underwatering could be the cause. Damage from underwatering would be preceded by wilting—an obvious symptom. So chances are that overwatering, or poor drainage which results in water accumulation in the soil, is the cause. Too much or too frequently applied fertilizer could also damage roots, causing the same symptoms. That sounds simple enough so far, but lack of light, insects, root diseases, and even certain fumes resulting from poor gas combustion could also cause those symptoms.

Another commonly observed symptom of houseplant problems is the tips or margins of leaves turning brown. This may occur when the plant repeatedly gets too dry but does not reach the point of wilting. Too much fertilizer could also produce that symptom. And a plant placed too close to a window during the winter may show that symptom because of cold injury.

If a plant seems to be producing smaller leaves than formerly, suspect insufficient light. However, small leaves could also be the result of lack of fertilizer or moisture, or even of excessively high temperature.

As a general rule, when a plant develops problems, you should check carefully for insects first, watering and fertilizing procedures second, and lastly the available light—intensity and duration.

In summary, then, select plants which can grow in the light conditions you can provide. Also select them in proportion to the position in which you wish to display them. Plan your plant care to maintain them—not for rapid growth. Be careful with plant watering.

You will notice that I have not told you to talk or sing to your plants. Nor do you need to be in love with them. A wholesale florist producing millions of plants each year would soon run out of words, music, or love! No scientific evidence exists indicating that any of those exotic treatments will help plants to grow. I suppose it might be possible that talking all day to a plant would increase the carbon dioxide content of the air around it and hence increase photosynthesis. That's a long shot, however. No, if you do your best to provide the correct growing conditions, plants will love you! But plants do die. The nice thing about plants is that you need feel no emotional attachment to them. If a plant dies, throw it away and start growing a new one.

GLOSSARY

Etiolation: The physical reaction of a plant to a reduction or absence of light, such as light-colored leaves or spindly stem.

Footcandle: A unit of measure for light intensity. .

Phototropism: The growth response of a plant to illumination from one side; bending of the stem or leaves toward the light.

Wick watering: A type of watering that uses some agent, such as a wick or sponge, to transfer water to the soil.

5

FOLIAGE AND FLOWERING PLANTS FOR THE HOME

This chapter deals with several small groups of plants which I think are easy to grow and which provide a range of foliage and flower types as well as a range of sizes and shapes. I do not mean to suggest that these are the "best" or "only" plants. I like them and have found them easy to grow. Among the foliage plants I shall discuss the tall ones first. All in this first group may be porpagated by cuttings or air layerings; a few may be started from seeds.

Croton (*Codiaeum variegatum*) is the most colorful of the foliage plants. Leaf colors include pink, red, yellow, white, and green. Leaves also vary in shape from one variety to another. New leaves are predominantly green and assume other colors as they age. This is a woody shrub or tree and will become a large plant, perhaps four to six feet tall and almost as wide. Because it needs direct sunlight, it should be placed near a south window; placed near an east or west window it *might* succeed. The soil should not be allowed to dry out completely. Warm temperatures are also a requirement for this plant, which means you have to be careful during the winter not to place it too close to the window. The croton is rather difficult to propagate. I recommend buying a small started plant and trying to grow it. If you fail, not much money will be lost. If you succeed, it will become a large plant in a few years. Lower leaves eventually fall in a natural process; the trick is to maintain the plant so new leaves will be produced.

Dizygotheca elegantissima is the scientific name of a plant formerly named aralia. Since that is a far easier name to remember, it is called false aralia. Fingerlike projections of the leaves, which have a reddish cast to them, provide unique foliage. This plant may be started from seed or cuttings; if necessary, it can also be air layered. A tall, narrow, woody plant, false aralia needs fairly bright light. Place it near a south, east, or west window. It can exist for

Houseplants: croton

months at a time with as little as 100 footcandles of light, but then it must be rehabilitated. Soil should be kept moist and not allowed to dry out. If the plant gets dry, the leaf tips will curl and turn brown. Seedlings of false aralia are sold for terrarium plants, but because they may reach six feet or more in height they are a dubious selection, or at least a short-term one.

Houseplants: false aralia

Dragon palm (*Dracaena marginata*) requires the same growing conditions as the false aralia. This plant is one you will see on movie sets, in home decorating magazines, and on television. Generally two or three plants of different ages are placed in a container. This plant assumes grotesque shapes. Lower leaves regularly fall off or are pulled off so that only a tuft of foliage about twelve inches long remains at the tip of the stem. The leaf scars from the missing leaves make the stem look like a palm although it is not a real palm. Then, to make it more interesting, one or two of the plants (before combining them in the final planter) may be allowed to respond phototropically to a single light source. The stems eventually harden in this bent position. Sometimes two or three bends are formed in each stem. When they are combined in a single container, the results are spectacular.

Houseplants: Dracaena marginata (*dragon palm*)

Houseplants: rubber plant

Figs (*Ficus*) are an interesting group of tall house-plants. Most of the group have large, shiny leaves. Included in this discussion are rubber plant, banyan tree, and fiddle leaf fig. Under the name rubber plant are a number of species and varieties which have the same general appearance but some differences in leaf colors. Some can be started from seed. The usual growth habit is a tall, slender, nonbranching plant. Since about 100 footcandles of light will keep it alive

Houseplants: banyan tree

(although more light will permit more growth), it is not necessary to place the plant near a window. Soil should not dry out. Chilling temperatures or cold drafts will cause the lower leaves to drop as will over- or underwatering.

The banyan tree in its native India will grow more than a hundred feet high. Its branches produce **aerial roots** which hang to the ground. Occasionally these roots produce a new stem where they have struck the ground, and a new tree results. Over a long period of time a clump of banyan trees can spread and move across the countryside. In a pot in your living room, however, the plant probably will not branch and will look and grow much like the rubber plant. The banyan tree is seldom sold commercially, but you can buy the seeds and grow it yourself. Growing requirements are the same as for the rubber plant.

Fiddle leaf fig has broad fiddle-shaped leaves. *Ficus lyrata*, the scientific name for fiddle leaf fig, is a rugged-looking plant. It seems more suited to a den or along wood-paneled walls than any of the other tall plants. While it needs a little more light than the

Houseplants: fiddle leaf fig

other figs, at 100 footcandles it will probably survive for several months. I would place it within six or eight feet of an east or west window. As with the other figs, keep the soil moist.

Dieffenbachia comprises several different species of large-leaved plants which will exist under poor light conditions. Even as little as 25 footcandles of light is enough for a year if the light duration is extended to sixteen hours each day. Given 100 footcandles or more, it should last almost indefinitely. The common name is dumb cane, because a bite of the stem or leaf

Houseplants: dieffenbachia

will cause the tongue to swell painfully and restrict the power to speak. Presumably, eating a large amount might be fatal, but it is hard to see how you could get by the first bite. Spurted into your eye, this same chemical may cause temporary blindness. Frankly, in my long association with horticulture I have never known or heard of anyone so afflicted. The dieffenbachia is a tropical jungle plant and grows under the cover of other plants in its native habitat. Warm, moist conditions seem to be best for it. In our homes it is difficult to keep the humidity high; as a result, lower leaves eventually drop off. New growth continues to push out, however. After a year or two in the home, dieffenbachia usually needs to be air layered to improve its appearance. While many pamphlets recommend heavy watering and allowing the soil to become quite dry between waterings, my own experience has been that letting the soil become dry can be a mistake. Actually this plant can be grown in water alone for six months or more. I think you are not likely to hurt it by overwatering.

Australian umbrella tree is also known as schefflera or, more correctly, *Brassaia actinophylla*. It may grow to be over six feet. I believe it will stand more abuse and lack of care than any other of the large plants. It may be started from seed, cuttings, or air layering. After a thorough watering the soil should be allowed to become quite dry; the leaves may droop but will rise again after watering. If kept too moist, the root system will be damaged permanently. This plant will grow, or at least live, in very little light (25 footcandles). The plant may not look the same as one grown in bright light, but it will survive. In bright light (near some window) it will produce many leaves with short internodes and will become perhaps two to three feet wide. Grown under poor light conditions it

Houseplants: schefflera

will be a much wider plant (four to five feet) with few leaves and much longer internodes. In either case, it will be an attractive addition to your home.

There are some vining plants we can include in the tall plant category. These plants have large leaves and need to be supported on some type of pole. Their ultimate height depends upon the height of the pole which supports them.

The supporting poles can be simple stakes of wood or bamboo. More attractive support posts may be purchased which are made of osmunda fiber or tree fern; or you can make or buy poles made of a cylinder of hardware cloth stuffed with sphagnum moss. Some commercial poles are made of chicken-wire cylinders stuffed with sphagnum moss, through which are run several heavy metal wires or stakes to add structural strength. Still another type of pole sold in plant stores is just a slab of wood with bark on one side. Any of these may be used. The trick is to train the plant to grow on them. Eventually the plant will attach itself to the supporting pole, but first you must fasten the plant stem to the pole. You might use florists' pins, which look like hairpins, or twist ties (a piece of wire covered with paper), or very soft twine. Or you *may* succeed in just winding the stem around the post.

Split leaf philodendron is a large-leaved vining plant. The first leaves produced on a new plant may resemble the common philodendron. As the stem lengthens and new leaves are produced, the leaves develop splits or holes. A plant a few years old old will have leaves full of holes, like Swiss cheese— which is sometimes used as a common name. When the stem reaches the top of the supporting post, allow it to bend back downwards and continue to elongate. I start it growing back upwards by pinning it to the pole again. After five or six years of this type of treatment, you will have a very bushy tall plant. Don't be alarmed if some of the leaves produced after it begins to grow downwards do not have holes in them. Apparently position has some effect on the production of holes in the leaves. Research has indicated that nutrition and the amount of available light may have a similar effect. Stem eye cuttings or air layering are propagation methods which can be used with this plant. A light source of 100 footcandles is sufficient.

Houseplants: split leaf philodendron

That amount of light will also support a spade leaf philodendron. *Philodendron hastatum* and its many **clones** and hybrids provide a variety of leaf shapes and colors. All the plants produce leaves up to twelve or fifteen inches long.

Fiddle leaf philodendron produces large leaves if given bright light. But if it is grown with only 100 footcandles of light, the leaves will be only four to six inches long. The unusual shape of the leaves, indicated by its name, make it an attention-drawing plant.

Houseplants: spade leaf philodendron

All three of these vining types need to be watered thoroughly and then watered again before the soil becomes completely dry.

It is possible to grow any of these foliage plants in a dark corner of your home if you will move them to a brightly lighted spot during the weekdays. But, because they are so heavy, you are not likely to move them. A solution is to buy a plant **caddy**, or trailer— simple pots or trays with concealed wheels or rollers under them. The caddies may be made of wood, metal, or plastic; many are quite attractive. By grow-

Houseplants: fiddle leaf philodendron

ing big plants on these movable platforms you can wheel them easily to lighted positions during the week or during the day and push them back into display positions when you wish, allowing most plants to be kept healthy and still be displayed artistically. If in doubt about the adequacy of your light supply, this is a sure way to grow plants successfully.

Not everyone can use tall plants, for they require large open areas for display. The following plants are of small to medium size, seldom exceeding three feet in height.

Chinese evergreens include a number of different species of *Aglaonema*. As a group they are not fussy about the amount of light they receive. They will grow nicely in bright light; better yet, they will also live with very little light. If you can read by the light they receive, and if that amount of light is available to them fifteen to sixteen hours each day, these plants will last in your home for several years. Whereas most plants are quite sensitive to the amount of water they receive and the frequency of watering, these are not. Of course, you can underwater them and lose

Houseplants: Chinese evergreen

Houseplants: Chinese evergreen

them.   Few plants can go without water for long, but these seem to stand overwatering better than most. They prefer a damp soil.   In fact, they can be grown in water—without soil.

If these plants receive bright light, they may flower. The flowers are unusual but not pleasing.   Eventually, however, some attractive pea-sized fruits may appear, ranging in color during maturation from green to yellow to red.   The large, smooth leaves of Chinese evergreens may be plain green or have yellow or gray

Houseplants: Chinese evergreen

patterns interspersed with varying shades of green. Some look like miniature dieffenbachias, to which they are fairly closely related. In addition to stem cuttings and air layering, propagation of Chinese evergreens by stem eye cuttings will also succeed.

Several philodendrons are not climbing nor vining types. These produce huge leaves which are deeply cut like the split leaf philodendron. Cut leaf philodendrons like *Philodendron selloum* or *P. minarum* will not grow very tall but are quite wide plants. They thrive on warm, moist conditions and, while they do best in bright light, will exist for months with only 100 footcandles of light. You can buy seeds of *P. selloum*, but I have found them difficult to germinate.

Houseplants:
cut leaf philodendron

Peperomias, a group of plants from the pepper family, have proved themselves excellent houseplants, and a number of different species may be grown with ease. Some common ones are watermelon plant, Silver Heart, and Emerald Ripple. Many peperomias are used as terrarium plants, for all remain rather small and most will endure poor light conditions. But they really prefer dry soil. Water them thoroughly but allow them to become very dry before the next watering.

Cast iron plant (*Aspidistra elatior*) was a favorite in the 1890s and the early part of this century. So resistant to neglect that it would endure the dim light, smoky air, and infrequent watering provided by tavern owners of that time, it became known as the saloon plant. A song was even popular which extolled the plant. Perhaps it was too common to be grown in more "proper" environments, such as the home, for it virtually disappeared from the houseplant scene. But it is coming back. A white-striped version is also now available. And, if you give the cast iron

Houseplants:
Peperomia obtusifolia
(*common peperomia*)

Houseplants:
Emerald Ripple peperomia

plant enough light, it will produce the most unusual flowers right on the soil surface, seemingly not attached to the plant at all. About the size of silver dollars, these flowers appear to be carved out of wood. The plant itself consists of a number of large leaves which emerge from an underground stem. It's a tough old bird.

Toughest of all the plants, with one exception, is one called snake plant, or bowstring hemp, or mother-in-law's tongue. *Sansevieria trifasciata* and related species are hard to kill. An unauthenticated story illustrates how tough they are. A woman received one as a housewarming gift when she moved into a new home. She didn't like the plant, but rather than obviously throwing it away, she placed it in the basement. There it sat unattended. Three years later she moved to a new address and the movers, being very thor-

Houseplants: watermelon plant

Houseplants: cast iron plant

Houseplants: mother-in-law's tongue

Houseplants: cylindrical sansevieria

ough, brought the plant out of the basement looking about the same as it had three years before! An exaggeration? Perhaps.

About 25 footcandles of light will do for this sansevieria, but full sunlight is all right too. It can grow in water with no soil but, strangely, may rot if you water it too frequently. Underwatering this plant is almost impossible.

Other species in this genus are almost as tough. *Sansevieria hahnii*, or rosette sansevieria, is a dwarf form. Cylindrical sansevieria requires more light but will stand hot, dry conditions. Its long, cylindrical leaves are stiff and sharply pointed. If you are tired of the ubiquitous mother-in-law's tongue, you might try one of these others.

Foliage begonias, like the many rex begonias and iron cross begonia, are more demanding in their care requirements, but their many leaf variations are a welcome addition to the houseplant collection. These plants need to be grown *near* an east or west window or under artificial lights where around 500 footcandles of light will be available at least part of each day. They cannot stand direct sunlight for more than half a day. The key to growing these plants successfully is to provide high relative humidity. Suggestions for raising relative humidity were presented earlier in this chapter.

Let me conclude the list of foliage plants by mentioning a few of the easy-to-grow vining plants that have small leaves and stems that hang or trail from the pot, displaying the foliage. These plants may be placed on shelves, bookcases, in hanging baskets, in wall brackets, and so on.

Grape ivy (*Cissus rhombifolia*) is not my favorite plant, but it will grow without direct sunlight and may

Houseplants: Rex begonia

Houseplants: Iron Cross begonia

Houseplants: grape ivy

become an almost bushy type of vine. If watered frequently and given adequate light, it will take over your living room.

Arrowhead vine (*Syngonium podophyllum*) is called nephthytis by most florists. Several variegated versions also exist, such as Emerald Gem and Tri-leaf Wonder. The leaves of most are shaped like an arrowhead. The petioles grow extremely long and give the unfortunate effect of putting more space between leaves. The plant will soon spill downward from the pot. It requires very little light and some varieties may be started from seed.

Houseplants: arrowhead vine

Houseplants:
arrowhead vine

Philodendron (*P. oxycardium*) is probably the most popular foliage plant. Started from cuttings, it will grow in very little light. It will also grow in a glass of water. When grown in soil it prefers moist rather than dry conditions but will not survive if watered too frequently. Philodendron is one of the easiest houseplants to grow. Devil's ivy (*Scindapsus aureus*), also called pothos, ranks with mother-in-law's tongue in toughness. It can almost survive in the dark. Over- or underwatering may discourage it but seldom kill it. The plant may lose a few leaves but new growth will continue. Where the old leaves have been lost because of improper care, long bare stems remain. I simply wind these around the pot in long, loose loops so that sections of stem bearing leaves will cover up the bare-looking portions. Stem cuttings or stem eye cuttings will root even in water if no rooting medium is available. In fact, the plant can be grown in water.

Houseplants: common philodendron

If you are just starting to grow houseplants, or if you have repeatedly failed to grow them, try growing devil's ivy and mother-in-law's tongue. If you kill them, try plastic plants!

Flowering plants for the home are more difficult to grow than foliage plants because they require much more light. The flowering plant which will survive with the *least* amount of light is the African violet (*Saintpaulia ionantha*). Even it, however, must have

Houseplants: devil's ivy

about 600 footcandles of light, about the amount that will exist directly before a north window most of the year. Even that position won't be lighted enough during December and January. On the other hand, you can damage this plant with too much light. Placed in a south window during the summer, the African violet leaves will burn. Pink, white, and blue are the usual flower colors. Flowers are produced in waves, with a three or four week period of heavy flowering and then six weeks or so with no flowers. Watering becomes a problem because the foliage of the African violet often completely covers the soil

Houseplants: African violet

surface. The leaves will become discolored when water droplets stand on them, forming irregular yellow circles. Room temperature water is less apt to cause discoloring than cold water, but even it may do damage. Probably the best way to water these plants is to use the immersion system or grow them in some type of wick watering container. This type of container also adds humidity to the air around the plant and African violets thrive on high humidity. In fact, the best rooms in which to grow them are the kitchen and the bathroom. Leaf cuttings are used for propagation.

Gloxinias (*Sinningia speciosa*) should be grown directly before an east or west window. Propagation is accomplished by leaf cuttings, seeds, or tubers. A plant with large green leaves and unusual flowers, it is a relative of the African violet. It, too, prefers high humidity. The color range of the flowers extends from white to red to blue. Like the African violet it will produce flowers for awhile and then rest. In fact, most varieties actually go dormant. The leaves will begin to turn yellow, and you will think you have killed it. But the plant just needs to rest for a few months. Quit watering the gloxinia when this hap-

Houseplants: gloxinia

pens. The leaves will all fall off. It will just sit there and look dead for six or eight weeks. One day you will see new growth starting from the soil. Then put the plant back in the window and begin watering.

Vining violets (*Episcia*) are another relative of the African violet. Sometimes they are called hanging African violets. They frequently have very colorful foliage although some varieties have green leaves. Flower colors range from white to yellow to red. The distinguishing feature of these plants is the production of runners which hang down around the pot. The runners will have miniature plants (plantlets) formed at intervals along them. Flowers may appear on these as well as on the plant in the pot. They are not, however, prolific flower producers.

Vining violets require about as much light as the gloxinia so they should be grown near an east, west, or south window. The south window may provide too much light in the summer. Propagation is accom-

Houseplants: vining violet

Houseplants: vining violet

Houseplants: vining violet

plished by putting the little plantlets, either attached to or detached from the runners, into a rooting medium.

Two flowering garden plants will grow in the home. Patience plant (*Impatiens sultanii*) and the wax begonia (*Begonia semperflorens*) do fairly well indoors. They prefer rather high relative humidity, which is sometimes difficult to provide in our well-heated but dry houses. Both are propagated by means of seeds or stem cuttings. Both need direct sunlight for at least a few hours each day. Patience plant has a wider range of flower colors, but the wax begonia may provide red, green, or variegated leaf colors. These plants flower almost continuously.

Houseplants: patience plant

Houseplants: wax begonia

Many other flowering plants purchased from the florist in full bloom should be enjoyed while they continue to flower but should be discarded when the flowers are gone. Such plants include chrysanthemums, poinsettias, Easter lilies, cinerarias, and azaleas. These all require special combinations of temperature, day length, light intensity, and timing. They do not grow well in the home and were never intended to be true houseplants. I call them "gift" plants. Keep them moist, away from direct sunlight, and enjoy them while they are attractive. It is possible, but not probable, that you can urge them to flower again. And they will never be as nice looking as when you bought them.

If you have a greenhouse or a well lighted and heated sun room or even a south-facing picture window, then you can grow many more flowering plants.

Houseplants: chrysanthemum

Houseplants: poinsettia

Houseplants: azalea

For most of us, however, light is the limiting factor in selecting houseplants. Flowering plants simply require a lot of light.

Really impressive houseplant displays in the home will include five or six plants grouped together along a wall or in a corner with tall, medium, vining, and flowering plants all represented. Not only is this an attractive display, but the plants will grow better because of the increased humidity from moist soil and transpiration.

Houseplants: corner display

GLOSSARY

Aerial root: Roots that develop above ground on some plants.

Caddy: A movable platform on which large plants may be placed to enable them to be easily moved.

Clone: A group of plants produced by a sexual or vegetative propagation from a single original plant.

Variegated: Having many colors in streaks or spots.

*

6

CONTAINER GARDENING

Having studied the care and conditions necessary for growing individual houseplants, you should now be ready to advance to container gardening. In a broad sense container gardening includes landscapes for rooftops, malls, airports, and offices. Our discussion, however, will be restricted to container gardening in and around the home.

Gardening both indoors and out in pots, tubs, planters, window boxes, or other containers has become very popular during the last few years. Many people now live in apartments, townhouses, and condominiums, and they do not have the ground space necessary for ordinary gardening. The alternative is to grow flowers, foliage plants, trees, shrubs, and vegetables in various types of containers.

In order to place several plants attractively in a single container, some knowledge of the principles of arranging is necessary. We can look to flower arranging for the basic concepts. Any acceptable flower (or plant) arrangement must follow some plan. The underlying shape should be some geometric form. About seven basic forms are used in flower arranging:

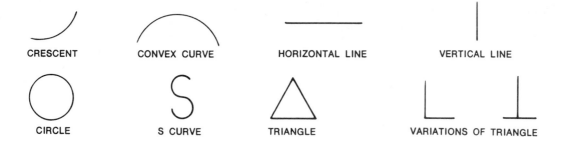

CRESCENT CONVEX CURVE HORIZONTAL LINE VERTICAL LINE

CIRCLE S CURVE TRIANGLE VARIATIONS OF TRIANGLE

The S curve and circle are seldom used in plant arranging.

The second rule we borrow from flower arranging is to provide an accent point in the plant grouping. Some plant should draw the eye to it. A focal point is necessary. Admittedly, we cannot always provide that point, for we may have only a few plants, none of which is unusual. But a plant that is quite different in appearance from the rest should be placed in the center of the curve or line or triangular arrangement. Lacking a startling accent plant, you may achieve a focal point by grouping a few plants closer together to create more "weight" at the point considered the center of the arrangement. Putting plants farther apart at the edges of the arrangement will tend to draw the eye to the thicker planting.

Thirdly, the finished container should look balanced. If it looks like it will tip over, you have not balanced it. It need not be symmetrically balanced, however. A tall plant placed at one side of the arrangement may be balanced by a number of smaller ones or even the expanse of a long container. You will be aware of an unbalanced appearance when the arrangement disturbs you; this means some plants need to be shifted.

Finally, the proportions of the plants and containers should match. Tall plants should not be placed in shallow containers. In other words, the ultimate dimensions of the plants must be considered when selecting the container. The height of the tallest plant in an arrangement should be restricted to one and one-half times the largest dimension of the container. A somewhat shorter plant may be used if it is a type that will elongate.

Indoor planters and room dividers are really just containers. Following the rules of flower arranging you should try to arrange plants in them in some pleasing combinations. But the important point is to keep the plants in pots. Do *not* fill the container with soil! Instead fill it with peat, sphagnum moss, or vermiculite. Plants growing in their pots may then be plunged in the planting medium. The advantage of this is that plants which fail to grow or which grow too rapidly may be removed and replaced without disturbing the roots of neighboring plants. In addition, you will not eventually have a sodden mass of disease-ridden soil, heavy and difficult to remove. Plant arrangement is also easier, and if the pots are plunged deeply they won't show.

Outdoor planters are another matter. Those that are part of the house are usually planted with evergreens which will live and grow for years with the amount of light available outdoors. Of necessity they must be planted in soil, and their roots must be free for expanded growth. Should the soil need to be replaced, it can be done outdoors without worrying about damaging carpeting or woodwork.

Since window boxes planted for summer display outdoors are only used for three or four months, it really doesn't matter which technique you use. But with all the outdoor light and ventilation, plants will grow faster and better if removed from their pots and planted in soil.

Most of you may have the urge at some time to buy or plant a dish garden, which is merely a small container holding several plants. The series of steps in making a dish garden is the same as for any other container planting:

1. Choose the container.
2. Choose the location in which you wish to display it.
3. Choose plants in proportion to the container and which will live with the amount of light available at the desired location.
4. Decide whether the container will be viewed from just one side or from all sides.
5. Arrange the plants using the principles of flower arranging. A one-sided arrangement may be preferable if the container is to be placed against a wall.

Dish gardens made up of cactus plants are attractive, but the nature of the plants imposes certain limitations. Cacti and other **succulents** are generally quite small and all are sun loving. These characteristics restrict location to a position with direct sunlight most of the day. They also restrict the choice of containers to a rather shallow (one and one-half to two inches) dish whose width will be limited by the height of the tallest plant available. Clay saucers intended to go under flowerpots make nice cactus gardens. An earthenware or stoneware dish will also serve nicely. Succulents prefer an open, sandy soil. A good soil mixture is 3 parts sand, 1 part soil, 1 part peat, 1 part perlite. Fill the container almost to the top with this soil mixture. As you add plants, the mound of soil in the center may actually be higher than the sides of the container. With most dish gardens, however, the soil level should be kept one-half inch below the top of the container.

Decide on the arrangement for your garden and then knock the plants out of their pots. If the soil ball around the roots is too big to plant in this shallow container, crumple the soil in your hand until it breaks down leaving just bare roots. Start planting by putting in the tall plant first. When the planting is complete, sprinkle more sand over the surface to make it look like a desert.

The secret to watering a cactus garden is to neglect it. If you underwater cactus plants, they begin to shrivel, but they will revive when watered. If you overwater them, they rot and die. So, water your garden after planting, put it in a warm, sunny spot, and forget it for several weeks. When you think it needs water, wait another week. Then use only half as much water as you think it needs.

An old idea revived in recent years is terrarium planting. Any clear glass or plastic container which can be closed or covered (but need not be) may be used. Colored or heavily etched glass, however, cuts out some light that is needed for plant growth. Be-

Houseplants: succulent

Houseplants: succulent

Houseplants: cactus

Houseplants: succulent

Houseplants:
variegated jade plant

Houseplants: cactus

Houseplants: cactus

*Cactus garden planted
with triangular design*

cause the plants in a terrarium are surrounded with glass, many people equate a terrarium with a greenhouse. Not so! A terrarium is really a miniature jungle floor. On a jungle floor the plants receive only filtered light, and the air and the soil are filled with moisture. In the jungle this moisture evaporates to form clouds which produce rain. Similarly, in a terrarium the moisture evaporates, condenses on the glass, and runs back down into the soil. The cycle is repeated indefinitely. If the container has no lid, some moisture escapes. Water will then have to be added. This does not mean you should keep the lid on all terrariums. For example, a short container will have so much condensation on the glass you won't be able to see the plants. This may even happen with a tall container but is less likely. I have a four-inch-tall terrarium with a lid on my desk. I leave it covered most of the time. Occasionally, however, I remove the lid for a few hours, and once every three or four months I add some water. But a nineteen-inch-tall bottle garden which could be closed with a cork has been left uncorked for as long as nine months without adding water.

Since a terrarium is a miniature jungle floor, you should select plants for it that do well in filtered light and moist surroundings. Slow-growing plants will live in the container longer. Fast-growing plants or those which prefer bright light and dry air will not last long. The plants in the accompanying list are appropriate for use in terrariums. After removing them from their pots, break down the soil ball and trim the roots (if needed) to fit into the container.

Ferns: *Pteris, Adiantum, Asplenium, Pellaea, Polystichum, Davallia, Cyrtomium*

Wandering Jew	English Ivy
Pellionia	*Fittonia*
Pilea	Palms
Ruellia	*Hemigraphis*
Creeping Fig	*Selaginella*
Prayer Plant	Bromeliads
Baby's Tears	Aluminum Plant
Boxwood	*Euonymus*
Rex Begonia	*Podocarpus*
Coleus	*Fatshedera*
African Violet	Schefflera
Peperomia	*Pittosporum*
Columnea	Chinese Evergreen
Episcia	*Dracaena*

One plant or several may be planted in a terrarium. A single African violet in a brandy snifter makes a delightful terrarium. More frequently several plants are planted together. The same rules apply to this type of plant arrangement as to any container planting. Admittedly, the actual planting is more difficult. With bottle gardens (which are terrariums) the narrow opening prevents hand planting. Special tools can be made or bought to be used as mechanical "hands." Several of these are pictured. When selecting the plants from your local greenhouse or garden center, pick plants of various heights. Choose one or two plants which are unusual to use as an accent point. And do not choose so many plants that they will be overcrowded.

Usable containers depend upon your imagination. Most popular today are fishbowls, brandy snifters, apothecary jars, water pitchers, cookie jars, and, of course, the many containers made especially for terrariums. But I have seen light bulbs, glass lamp

Terrariums:
a single plant, African violet,
displayed in a small terrarium

Terrariums:
a single plant, English ivy,
displayed in a small terrarium

Terrariums:
a single plant, arrowhead vine,
displayed in a small terrarium

*Terrariums: a single pilea
displayed in a small terrarium*

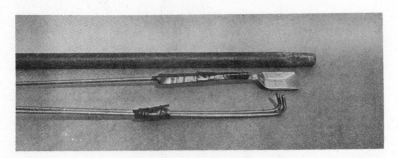

Terrarium tools

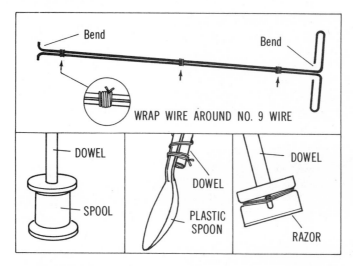

Terrarium tools

shades, mayonnaise jars, and other unusual containers used effectively. Bottles and jugs may also be used, but they are more difficult to plant.

Once again the same rules apply. Select the container, Determine the location or at least restrict the display area to one which does *not* receive direct sunlight, for sunlight shining on these nearly closed containers would raise the temperatures too high for plant life—the plants would literally cook. Select plants that will grow with indirect light or, at best, bright light and high humidity. Decide whether the container will be viewed from all sides or just one, and then plan your arrangement of plants according to the usual flower arranging principles. You will find it easier to put the big plant in last if it is to be placed directly beneath the opening.

In contrast to the usual planting advice, the bottom of the terrarium should be lined only with sphagnum moss. Most people use gravel in the bottom to pro-

Terrariums: a few of the many possible containers used as terrariums

*Terrariums: choose a design:
right angle, triangle, crescent*

*Terrariums: arrange plants
before you begin planting*

vide an area for water drainage if the soil is overwatered. Frequently the suggestion is also given to add charcoal in a layer over the gravel. Most people don't know why. Some will say it "sweetens" the soil. But it really won't do anything for the plants. The charcoal may absorb odors, but I have never found the aroma of a terrarium objectionable. In any case, the sphagnum moss will provide drainage. But, more practically, it will serve as an indicator for watering the terrarium. So long as the moss looks brown or dark in color, there is enough moisture in the terrarium. When the moss becomes tan or light in color, it has dried out, and the terrarium needs watering.

The depth of the total planting medium should not exceed one-fourth of the height of the container.

Terrariums:
line the container with sphagnum moss

Terrariums: place some soil in the center of the moss

With a shell of moss placed around the bottom and sides, soil can be added by making a depression in the center of the moss. Not much soil is really needed since it is there only to provide a source of nutrients for the plants. Even if the plants are not placed directly in the soil, their roots will eventually grow into it.

The soil ball around the roots of each plant may be too large to fit in the depth of rooting medium in the terrarium. If so, after the plant is knocked out of the pot, break the soil ball up with your fingers until only bare roots are present. You may even trim the roots if absolutely necessary. The conditions of light and humidity in a terrarium are such that roots will be replaced quickly. Cuttings without roots may even begin to root in this environment.

After the plants have been placed in their proper positions, the soil (or moss) must be pressed or tamped down to firmly position them. When all are

Terrariums:
insert plant in hole previously scooped out

Terrariums: in a bottle garden
the soil ball must be broken down
and a special tool used for planting

planted, they must also be watered. Probably the best method is to add small amounts of distilled water to the base of each plant by means of a meat baster. Or, distilled water sprayed from a squeeze bottle will do. Distilled water will not stain the glass or plants nor will it cause salt problems in the soil. Ordinary tap water is last choice and should be kept off foliage and glass. Overwatering is a very real danger with this type of planter. Once too much water is in the terrarium there is no way to remove it; the plants will die. So apply a little water at a time; allow a fifteen minute interval before adding more. When the moss looks dark or brown it has all the water it needs. Quit! It may be three weeks or three months or longer before you need to add more. Let the moss color be your guide.

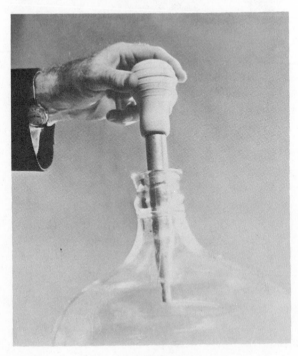

Terrariums:
watering may be done with a meat baster

Now enjoy your terrarium. Faster growing plants like coleus and baby's tears may have to be trimmed back or pruned. But aside from those chores nothing needs to be done but to enjoy. The planter should last for a year or two—more if you have done everything correctly.

The art of producing miniature trees which appear quite natural is called **bonsai**. This art began in China about the beginning of the fourteenth century. It spread to Japan where it had most of its development. Bonsai begins with a young woody tree or shrub which would normally become a huge plant, but by shaping and pruning, its growth is restricted to no more than forty inches. A bonsai may be a single plant, a multiple planting like a forest, or a group of stems forming a clump with only one root system. The trunk of these plants may be vertical but more frequently is bent to look windswept or even cascad-

Bonsai: materials necessary to start a bonsai

ing. The lower branches are removed to expose at least one-third of the trunk. If the trunk is to be bent, copper wire is spiraled up the stem so that the loops are one-half to two inches apart. The wire must be run through the drainage hole of the container and firmly anchored beneath the pot. Then the trunk is bent to the desired shape, and the wire holds it in position. After about three months, the wire must be removed or it will leave permanent grooves in the stem. By that time the woody stem will remain in its bent position.

Shaping the branches is next. Growth is restricted by pruning, and bending is done with wire if necessary.

Last to be shaped are the roots. The main or taproot is cut to force branch roots to form. Since we would like to have the tops of a few roots visible at the soil surface to create the impression of great age, when the plant is removed from the pot in which it has been trained, it may be replanted more shallowly, exposing a few roots.

The bonsai pots are the picture frames for this art. Shallow, dull-colored, usually plain pots with large drainages holes are used. The idea is to avoid distracting the viewer from his concentration on the plant. Also, a shallow pot has only a small area of soil available for root growth and thus helps to prevent the growth of bonsai plants. That also means watering daily with small quantities of water. The plants must be kept alive and healthy but must not be allowed to grow—a delicate balance. Continuous trimming and shaping is necessary, for bonsai culture is never finished. Some Japanese families have maintained a bonsai for more than four hundred years— each generation shaping, pruning, and caring for it.

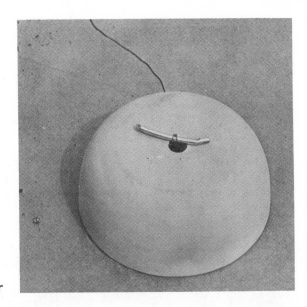

Bonsai: wire anchored through bottom of planter

Bonsai: young juniper being wired for training

Bonsai:
windswept appearance
of bonsai two months later

An old bonsai plant

Finally, you may wish to cover the soil with moss or gravel or add a rock or piece of wood as an interest point in the unnatural "natural" scene you have created. The plants used for bonsai have traditionally been outdoor plants; recently Americans have begun using some house plants. Pine, juniper, fir, azalea, and pyracantha, all with relatively small leaves, are the most commonly used plants for bonsai.

In water gardens, which are dish gardens without soil, plant arrangements can be very precise and compact. Using plants from the accompanying list, knock the plant out of the pot, loosen the soil with your fingers, and remove the final vestiges by washing the roots under water. Then simply impale the stem base and roots upon a florist's "frog," or pinholder, one of the holders used in ordinary flower arranging. The plants are easily shuffled around until a pleasing arrangement is achieved. Then add water until it covers all the roots. The water should be changed every three or four weeks. Fertilizer added to the water at about one-fourth the recommended amount will provide nutrients for continued growth. Even without fertilizer the plants should do well for about six months. The major problem is to prevent the buildup of algae or fungi in the solution which would ulti-

"Frog" for anchoring water garden

mately clog the vascular system or coat the roots, preventing entry of water into the plants. Using opaque containers helps prevent algal buildup. Metal containers are not recommended because the fertilizer solution may corrode the metal. An alternative to the florist's pinholder is the use of gravel, sand, or aquarium chips to provide anchorage and support for these bare-root plants.

Water Garden Plants

Chinese Evergreen	Arrowhead Vine
Coleus	*Philodendron*
Jade Plant	Mother-in-Law's Tongue
Dieffenbachia	Devil's Ivy
English Ivy	Wandering Jew
Red Ivy	

Plants suitable for a water garden can also be grown individually in bottles. Generally they are started as cuttings with the base of the stem in water in a narrow-necked bottle. Roots eventually form in the water, and the plant becomes fairly rigid while held in place between the root mass inside the bottle and the leaves outside.

Hanging baskets are another old-time favorite that has returned to popularity. Today's apartment or condominium dweller has limited floor space on the patio or porch. A way to increase the usable space is to hang containers along the walls or from the ceiling. This also serves to present the plants in a position at eye level where they appear to be different or certainly more noticeable.

*Houseplants: Chinese evergreen
planted in a water garden*

Finished water garden

Many types of hanging containers are available at your garden center today. Many more are possible if you use your imagination. Whatever type or size container you choose, remember these two points: a large container filled with wet soil is heavy and requires strong support; a suspended container dries out quickly. Lining the hanging basket with sphagnum moss will help to overcome both difficulties, but watering may become a daily or twice daily chore.

To start your hanging basket, place a shell of sphagnum moss one to two inches thick completely around the interior of the basket unless it is so small that weight will be no problem. Then place soil in the center. Finally, space your plants at intervals around the interface of soil and moss. Tip the plants at about a forty-five-degree angle so they have a better chance to hang over the edge of the container. One or more plants may need to be planted in the center to cover the soil. The plants should be pinched so that a number of stems will be produced by each plant.

Hanging baskets: line hanging container with a shell of sphagnum moss; place a small amount of soil in center

Hanging baskets: place plants around edge tipping them outward

Hanging baskets: completed planting has one or more plants in center as well

Your choice of plants is limited by the location in which the container is to be displayed. First of all, they should be trailing or hanging plants whose stems eventually hang after sufficient elongation. Plants with upright stems are better grown where they can be admired from above. The accompanying chart lists a few suggestions for hanging basket plants.

Hanging Basket Plants

A. Foliage (indoor or outdoor)

  1. Direct sun (south window)

      Burro's Tail (*Sedum*)
      Wax Plant
      Red Ivy

  2. Bright light (near an east, west, or north window)

Vining Violets	*Philodendron*
Sprenger's Asparagus	Devil's Ivy
Swedish Ivy	English Ivy
Wandering Jew	German Ivy
Airplane (Spider) Plant	*Pellionia*

B. Flowers (outdoors, greenhouse, sun porch)

  1. Direct sun

Rosary Vine	Weeping Lantana
Ivy Geranium	Shrimp Plant

  2. Partial shade (bright light; possibly grown indoors overwinter in south window)

      Browallia
      Impatiens
      Trailing Fuchsia

Hanging baskets:
hanging basket
several months later

As a conclusion to this section it should be pointed out that even some vegetables may be grown in containers. Peppers, cucumbers, and tomatoes may be grown in twelve-inch pots, boxes, or baskets. They need to receive direct sunlight most of the day and may need to be watered every day.

Some of the small-fruited varieties of pepper are decorative and still produce many hot peppers. Small-fruited tomatoes have been available for years. Now some patio-type tomatoes produce fruits two inches in diameter, but the plant will grow only about thirty inches high. The tomatoes will need to be staked or else a cylinder of concrete reinforcing wire may be placed inside the pot and the tomato plant will support itself on the wire. No pruning is necessary, and tomatoes may be picked and pulled through the large mesh openings. A few cucumber varieties are also now available to be grown the same way as tomatoes. The vines limit themselves in length to about twenty-four inches. Fruits are small—up to seven inches—but tasty. Beets, carrots, and lettuce also will grow in containers but are not really ornamental.

GLOSSARY

Bonsai: The art of producing miniature trees in a natural-appearing setting.

Succulent: Refers to plants that have enlarged stems or leaves capable of holding large amounts of water.

7

FLOWER GARDENS

Too often the inexperienced gardener buys plants or seeds because they appeal to him in the store or catalog but without regard to the location or need of his own garden. Then later he must decide where to put these plants. That gardener ends up with a hodge-podge garden. This is the reverse of the proper procedure. The correct way is to plan the garden first, then try to obtain the types and colors of flowers that will best fit the plan.

Flowers are usually planted in beds or borders. A flower bed is a planting that can be viewed from all sides; you can walk around it. Formal gardens are usually composed of individual flower beds. These gardens are not as popular today as they once were. Beds tend to appear rather stiff and formal. In today's informal living we prefer less stilted gardens. Flower borders are usually narrow gardens planted along a wall, a fence, or a row of shrubs; they are observable from only one side. Borders are usually limited to about five feet in width because they can be worked from only one side.

Before we discuss the area of design itself, perhaps we should study the soil preparation and necessary maintenance as well as some of the specific flowers we might choose.

Annuals, biennials and perennials are types of plants categorized by the life cycle they exhibit. **Annuals** are plants which may be started from seed and which produce foliage, flowers, and more seed all in one growing season. These plants die at the end of that season either from senescence or from freezing temperatures. They will not come up the following growing season. Some plants that we call annuals in the Midwest may be grown for years in a milder climate.

Biennials produce foliage the first season after seed germination but no flowers. During the second growing season new stems and leaves appear and, later, flowers and seeds. These plants die at the end of the second growing season. A few such garden biennials are foxglove, hollyhock, and pansy. We will not treat this group in further discussions of garden flowers for they are relatively few.

Perennials are plants which do not die even after flowering and continue to grow and flower year after year. They may or may not flower in the first season. Some perennials have herbaceous stems which are frozen to the ground each winter but are replaced the next spring by the root system, which lives year after year. Others are called woody perennials because their stems have a stronger structure that remains alive above ground over the winter.

Both annuals and perennials have advantages and disadvantages. All of the annuals may be started from seed, the cheapest means of propagation. Many perennials cannot be propagated that way or grow so slowly from seed that this method is not commonly used. So, economically, annuals have an advantage.

Annuals also have a flowering period considerably longer than that of most perennials. Most annuals flower continuously until frost kills them in the fall. Most perennials only flower during one part of the growing season. That may mean two, three, or more weeks. The true artist of the garden, however, will say this enables you to have a changing scene as the season progresses rather than the monotony of the same-colored flowers in the same place all summer.

The gardener may be inclined to believe that the selection among annuals is rather limited compared to the vast array of perennials available. Yet there is quite a range of sizes among annuals. Plants like lobelia, sweet alyssum, and portulaca are extremely small, but others will range up to shrub size as does summer cypress (*Kochia*), and the even taller cleome and castor bean and sunflower may reach six feet, or taller, in a single growing season.

Most annuals must be grown in full sunlight, but many perennials thrive in shady or partially shaded areas. So the light conditions might affect your choice of garden flowers. An obvious disadvantage to an annual garden is replanting each year, but this does present a chance to redesign your garden and correct mistakes. Actually, most gardens will combine annuals and perennials.

If you are starting a garden for the first time, there are certain physical and mental steps necessary. Let's take the physical steps first and look at soil preparation. Assuming no garden has been in this area before, lay out the design shape with string or mark it with sticks. Then skim off the sod or top one inch of lawn within the design area. Use the sod to patch bare places in the lawn, or throw it away. While it might seem that material turned under could provide "green" manure in the garden, usually it just provides a source of weeds as the unwanted grass plants continue to emerge in the newly formed garden. To supply the necessary organic matter, spread a one-inch layer of peat over the entire area. A common garden fertilizer should be added at this time, too, for it will be easier to apply uniformly when no plants are in the way. Directions on the bag will tell you how much to apply.

Annual plants have rather shallow root systems. To accommodate annuals, then, you need to work this area down only to a depth of about eight inches. A spading fork or shovel of any kind can be used to dig down, lift up, turn over, and break up the soil while mixing fertilizer and peat with the garden soil. The idea is to make sure no clods or lumps persist, we want a loose, open soil that will provide drainage and aeration for the depth of the root systems growing there. This soil preparation must be repeated each year.

A perennial garden, whose soil should be worked initially to a depth of fifteen inches, will receive this type of soil preparation only once. After that, plants which must not be disturbed will be growing there. Perennial plants growing in place year after year will develop much deeper root systems than annuals.

Maintenance of an annual garden is fairly simple. Water should be applied once each week unless it rains. The use of soil soaker hoses, which soak the soil without compacting it and without wetting the plant foliage, is recommended. While annuals can stand quite dry conditions, they will look much better if they receive sufficient water. Weeds, which are simply plants out of place, must be fought constantly, for they remove needed water and nutrients from the soil. Weeds may be discouraged by scratching the soil surface with a hoe about every ten days during the growing season. Annuals, remember, have roots near the soil surface so care must be taken not to **cultivate** too deeply. This shallow scratching of the soil also serves another purpose, preventing the formation of a hard, crusty surface on the garden soil. With the surface open and porous, water will penetrate more readily. Rainfall will then benefit all sections of the garden rather than running over the crust to the lowest spot. **Herbicides** are available to help fight the weeds, but they do not keep the soil surface open.

The other bit of maintenance necessary is removing old flowers. Food priorities in the plant are such that if seeds are being produced, surplus food will go into seed production. If flowers are being produced, but no seeds, food will be utilized in flower production. Should neither flowers nor seeds be forming, food will go into vegetative growth. Because we want flowers in the garden once the plants have become established, faded flowers should be removed to prevent seed formation and increase flower production.

Perennials demand a more elaborate maintenance program. You will have more money invested in them. In addition, they remain in place for years, so greater care must be given them than annuals, which live only for four or five months. Before growth starts in the spring is the time to cut fresh, sharp edges around the garden. This is also the time to press back into the soil any plants heaved up by the action of alternate freezing and thawing of the soil. Late in the winter in the Midwest, while the soil is frozen, a few warm, sunny days thaw out the top of the soil. It freezes again at night, sometimes pushing plants up so their roots are exposed. So long as the plants are dormant, little damage occurs. But after growth starts, the exposed roots will be damaged by exposure to sun and wind. Simply push them back down into the soil.

Stem and leaves which were frozen should be removed from the soil. Plant refuse may harbor disease organisms or insects. If this refuse is worked into the soil, the plant enemies which frequently overwinter get a fast start on new growth.

Soil cultivation and watering are necessary in this perennial garden, too. Perennials develop roots which penetrate more deeply into the soil than those of annuals, but I still recommend just shallow cultivation—only scratching the soil to a depth of one-half to one inch.

Fertilizing is more important for these plants than it is for annuals since you are building a permanent plant for year after year flower production. After the initial soil preparation and planting, fertilizing must be done on a regular schedule. A standard garden fertilizer (4-10-4, 4-8-6) should be applied twice each season. The first application should be made soon after growth starts in the spring, and a second application will be needed in early summer (July). Do not apply fertilizer late in the summer, because that encourages new, succulent growth at a time when frost danger is approaching. Roots or woody stems with new growth may be seriously damaged by early frosts. Apply fertilizer by spreading it as evenly as possible over the soil surface, being careful to keep it off the foliage. Then work the fertilizer into the soil with a rake or hoe and water it in.

Taller perennials, such as delphiniums or gladiolus or lilies, may need to be staked as a precaution against the possibility of wind damage.

Faded flowers should be removed just as was recommended for annuals. With most perennials there will be no increase in flower production the first year, but more sugar will be available for new vegetative growth leading to greater flowering the next season.

Mulching may prove to be the most important thing you do for your garden. A mulch is a two-inch or three-inch layer of some material, usually organic but not always, spread evenly over the garden soil. This may be some type of hull (buckwheat hulls, cottonseed hulls, etc.), ground corncobs, grass clippings, leaves, hay, manure, peat, pine needles, sawdust, straw, wood chips, even gravel or clay chips. Such a mulch in the summer may save the gardener considerable time and effort. First, it helps to conserve moisture in the soil by preventing evaporation from the soil surface. Similarly, it will prevent "crusting" of the soil. As an insulating blanket, it will keep soil temperatures cooler during the hot summer afternoons, encouraging more root growth. In addition, this blanket of mulch will prevent germination of most weed seeds, for they will be buried too deeply to begin growth. And, if you have used an organic material, it will gradually meld with the soil and be a constant replenishment of that precious commodity in the soil.

A winter mulch also serves several purposes. Not only is it a source of organic matter for the soil, it serves an important insulating function. It will help to prevent soil temperatures from falling quite as low as they might otherwise. The difference in temperature may be only a degree or two at the fifteen-inch depth, but research has shown that a degree or two can mean the difference between life and death for root systems of a number of perennial plants. The second purpose a winter mulch accomplishes is to prevent thawing of the upper soil areas during the occasional thaws on bright, warm days in late winter. With a mulch the ground will stay frozen even on a sunny afternoon, preventing the alternate freezing and thawing of the soil that leads to plant upheaval. Areas of the country which always have a heavy snow cover during the winter have a natural winter mulch. Even there, however, the application of an additional mulch before the snow flies will help.

The last part of our suggested maintenance program is least important. It won't make or break your garden. From time to time you may need to replace plants or divide them because they have outgrown their designated area. Without a plan gaps of large proportions may appear throughout your garden in some years. You might want to adopt a renovation program by dividing your garden into five or six areas of about equal size and renovating one of them each year. This is done best in the fall after plants have become dormant following several killing frosts. At that time of year even the bulbs can be dug. This type of program will confine the gaps or thin areas to one small area of the garden each year.

Planning a garden, whether annual or perennial, is a difficult but necessary process. Choosing a location and designing an outline or shape for the garden will be the same for annuals and perennials. The location should receive direct sunlight at least one-half of the day. Annuals do better if they are in full sun all day. However, a few annuals and many perennials can grow in partially shaded locations. The area should drain well, too. You can test the potential drainage by digging a hole about ten inches deep with a trowel and then filling it with water. After the water has drained away, refill the hole with water. Drainage is adequate if the water disappears within eight hours after the second fill. If drainage is not good and no other location is possible, don't give up hope. Additional preparation, costing both time and money, can make the area suitable. One possibility is to install drain tiles at about a two-foot depth. A less permanent way is to spread a six-inch layer of gravel at the base of the area about two feet below the surface. Some improvement may also be made by mixing sand into the soil. Raising the garden above the surrounding ground by trenching around the garden and tossing that soil on the garden will help. Drainage is important!

Curved gardens
before planting

*Curved gardens
before planting*

*Curved gardens
at the end of the season*

*Curved gardens
at the end of the season*

Most people are inclined to plant rectangular gardens whose straight lines and right angles match those of their property lines, driveway, sidewalk, or house. Dull! More imaginative designs may be created with gently curving lines. Broad sweeping curves are more restful to the eye and easier to maintain. No one will notice if your garden edges aren't quite straight or neat if the edge is a curve, but a deviation in a straight line is obvious. A small garden at one corner of your yard could be a gentle curve. Or a more ambitious gardener might use one side and the back of the yard in a series of long sweeping curves.

Selecting plants is the final step in planning your garden. Here we had better discuss annuals and perennials separately. Let's look at annuals first. The accompanying chart lists the more common, easy-to-grow annuals.

Petunias are the most popular mainstay of the garden. They provide massive displays of flowers all summer. Multiflora petunias produce many small flowers and are most often used to supply the bulk of the color in an annual garden. Grandiflora petunias have larger but fewer flowers. Both multiflora and grandiflora types have varieties listed as "doubles." That means they have more than one set of petals—a more "full" flower. Flower production is usually less with double types.

Geraniums are the only annuals which are commercially produced by cuttings as well as by seeds. They are the most expensive of the annuals and, for that reason, are usually kept in containers or limited areas of the garden. But they do provide a brilliant flower display in a sunny location.

Color Mass (12"–15" spacing)	Edging (6"–8" spacing)	Shade (12"–15" spacing)
Petunia	Sweet Alyssum	Impatiens
Marigold	Ageratum	Coleus
Zinnia	Portulaca	Wax Begonia
Celosia	Dwarf Marigold	
Snapdragon	Dwarf Zinnia	
Geranium		

The annuals called edging plants are all quite small and look best as a border for a garden, where they will not be covered up by taller plants.

Most of the annuals on the list prefer a warm, sunny location. Very few will do well or produce many flowers if they receive much shade; the exceptions are listed in the chart. Impatiens will grow and flower on the north side of your house even though they never receive direct sunlight. Coleus is grown for its colorful foliage, so we are not interested in its rather inconspicuous flowers. The foliage grows nicely in shaded locations. Wax begonias will survive in partially shaded areas. They grow better in direct sunlight of long duration but will survive so long as they get some sun each day.

You will have to look through a florist's shop or seed catalog and decide what plants you want. A small garden should not be a hodgepodge of colors or plant types, but a concentration on one or two colors repeated with different plant heights. Draw up a scale plan of your garden. Using a plastic or tracing paper overlay, sketch in with irregular circles the various groups of plants. Small border plants may be indicated by just one elongated ellipse representing, say, one color of sweet alyssum. Taller plants, naturally, belong toward the back of the garden. Each circle represents a group of plants since we seldom, if ever, plant one of a kind. You might even color in your rough design to get a better idea of how it would look. This is the time to change your mind—before you begin spending money.

Having decided on the assortment of plants, you must then decide whether to start them from seeds, either indoors in containers or outdoors directly in the garden area you planned for them, or to buy them already started from a garden center or florist's shop. My recommendation is to start them indoors from seed (chapter 2). If you plant them outdoors by seed, sow them in rows so when they come up you can tell them from weeds. Flowers and weeds all look alike at first. Seeds can't be placed outdoors before May because the soil will be too cold, and if they emerge too early, they may be killed by frost. Seeds must be covered by one-fourth to one-half inch of fine soil or sand to prevent them from being washed away by rain, blown away, or eaten by birds. Eventually young seedlings must be thinned so the plants will be properly spaced.

The more expensive alternative is to buy started plants from the garden center or florist. Do not be influenced by flowers on the plants; look instead for plants which have several branches, much foliage, and preferably no flowers. These plants will have sufficient photosynthetic area to produce the extra sugar necessary for continuous flowering. Plant them in slightly moist soil at the same depth or slightly deeper than they were planted in the pots. A saucer-shaped depression should exist around the plant so that water will run off the surrounding area to the plant, providing more water immediately beneath the stem. This will help to supply adequate water during the shock period that accompanies transplanting. If the plants you buy are in clay or plastic pots, you must take them out of the pots to plant them in the soil. This is done by putting your fingers over the soil and around the stem and inverting the pot, then with a sharp downward movement strike the edge of the pot on a step or fence post. Lacking some sturdy upright object on which to strike the pot, a stick or tool handle may be used to tap the edge of the pot. Peat pots can be dropped directly into the soil; they will eventually decompose. You should make sure the peat pot is completely buried in soil, and it is a good idea to crumple the upper edges of the peat pot, too, to be sure it will decompose rapidly. Should you fail to take these precautions with peat pots, the exposed edge of the pot will act like a wick. Moisture will be drawn from around the plant roots and evaporated from the exposed pot causing the plants to wilt even though the surrounding soil seems moist.

Planning a perennial garden is a more complex operation. We need to know more about the plants. For example, most perennials only flower for a short period; many become unattractive after flowering or even disappear from sight. I suggest you make a list of perennial plants you would like to have in your flower garden by looking through catalogs, talking with gardening friends, or trying to remember someone else's garden. Then divide this list into four groups representing different periods of the growing season—spring, late spring, summer, late summer. You will have to do a little research here. Catalogs and library books on gardening should supply information on when during the season you can expect each plant to flower and whether it will remain a green, attractive plant after flowering. List each of the plants under its correct flowering time. Then subdivide each of the four lists into tall, medium, and short groups to ensure proper placement of plants in the garden, so that short plants are not hidden by taller ones.

Some more advanced gardeners might further subdivide these lists by flower color, leaf color, and even leaf texture to assure that clashing colors or textures will not occur side by side in the garden. But that is probably a bit complicated for a beginning gardener.

A plastic overlay placed on a scale plan of the garden is helpful at this stage. First sketch in rough circles representing the earliest-flowering plants. Distribute them throughout the garden, paying attention to size differences as we mentioned earlier when discussing annuals. Then check the column representing late spring flowering plants and distribute those over your garden plan. Continue this until you have entered all the plants. Later you must determine how many of each kind you need to fill the space allocated to it. If plants disappear after flowering, you can either cover those spaces with other perennials or plant annuals. The end result will be a garden which presents a constantly changing scene as the growing season progresses. You cannot achieve this by accident. It is the result of planning.

Because perennials are planted at many different times of the year and there are so many of them, it might help to look at a brief listing of some of the "sure fire" perennials for the Midwest. They are presented in the order of their flowering from early spring until late summer. All need at least one-half day of direct sunlight each day unless otherwise noted.

Name	Planting Method/Time	Flowering Time	Comments
Crocus	Corms/3″ deep/Oct., Nov.	March, April	
Narcissus	Bulbs/4″–6″ deep/Oct., Nov.	March, April	
Tulips	Bulbs/4″–6″ deep/Oct., Nov.	April, May	
Creeping Phlox	Divisions/Spring	April, May	Full sun
Iris	Rhizomes/1″ deep/July, Aug.	May, June	
Lily-of-the-Valley	Rhizomes (pips)/April	May, June	Shade
Peony	Tuberous root/top no deeper than 2″/Aug., Sept.	June	
Delphinium	Seed or seedling/April	June, July (maybe again in Sept.)	
Daylily	Tuberous root/2″–4″ deep/anytime	July	
Phlox	Divisions/April, May	July, Aug.	
Lily	Bulb/6″–8″ deep/Oct., Nov.	July, Aug.	
Hosta	Divisions/April (or anytime)	Aug.	Shade
Chrysanthemum	Division/April, May	Sept., Oct.	

To this list we can add a few "tender" perennials. Tender perennials are plants that must be dug in the fall before the ground freezes, or they will be killed; but the reproductive structure can be saved from year to year.

Name	Planting Method/Time	Flowering Time	Comments
Canna	Rhizome/May	Continuous	Full sun
Gladiolus	Corm/May, June	80–90 days after planting	Full sun
Tuberous Begonia	Tuberous root/May	Continuous	Shade
Caladium	Tuber/May	Foliage display	Shade

Because these are tender perennials, they will need to be dug in the fall and stored over the winter. Each requires a little different storage process. Cannas are dug after frost kills the tops. Dry the plants on a porch or sidewalk for several days; cut off the stems, shake the soil off the rhizomes and store them on trays, newspapers, or in well-ventilated boxes at 50° to 60° F.

Gladiolus should be handled in the same way except they are put in a ventilated bag or box and stored at 40° to 45° F. Refrigerated storage or possibly an attic should work fine.

Tuberous begonias and caladiums are usually covered with vermiculite in bags or boxes and stored at 40° to 45° F.

All of these tender perennials except the gladiolus will give you more garden pleasure if you start them indoors planted shallowly in sand or vermiculite about March 1. After they start to grow, they should be transplanted into individual pots. Started in this manner, they will begin flowering soon after they are planted outdoors and will continue the rest of the summer. Tuberous begonias and caladiums will do better if planted in a very acid medium like peat.

Perennials provide us with a tremendous amount of variation in plant size, required growing conditions, flowering time, and so forth. This has been but a cursory introduction to that type of gardening.

GLOSSARY

Annuals: Plants which flower and die in a single growing season.

Biennials: Plants which normally produce shoots but not flowers during the first growing season, and produce more shoots, flowers, and die during the second season.

Cultivate: To scratch the soil to loosen the surface and to remove weeds.

Herbicide: Chemicals which destroy plants. Some kill all vegetation, others are selective.

Mulch: A layer of some material placed over the soil to reduce evaporation, control weeds, and modify soil temperature.

Perennials: Plants which do not die after flowering but continue to live for many seasons.

*

8

VEGETABLE GARDENS

Flower gardening stirs most people's esthetic sense, but vegetable gardening arouses the practical person in us. The idea of independence achieved by growing one's own food, even a small part, is appealing. Children are fascinated by the process of planting a seed, watching its growth, and eating the resulting product.

Vegetable gardening is similar to flower gardening but has the additional problem of harvesting the crop at the correct time. Harvesting is crucial if you want vegetables which will taste better than those bought in the store. If you put a dollar value on the hours you will spend working with vegetables, you probably will not save money. If you have the time, enjoy working with plants, and appreciate quality vegetables, then your efforts will be worthwhile.

Preparation of the soil is the same as for an annual garden. Maintenance includes cultivating (weeding), watering, fertilizing, and controlling pests. Avoiding periods of water shortage is even more critical with vegetables than with flowers. Do not let the plants dry out; this may mean watering some of them every other day. So far, vegetable growing sounds like flower gardening. The best location would receive full sun all day although a minimum of six hours will produce vegetables.

Just a few of the easier-to-grow vegetables will be discussed here. Let's look first at those you should start indoors. Lettuce, cabbage, peppers, and tomatoes can be planted in your home, just like the annual flower seeds, about six to eight weeks before frost danger has passed. When they develop true leaves, transplant them into individual pots and give them all the sunlight you can find. After the last average frost date has passed, transplant them into your garden area. They should be spaced about two feet apart in all directions.

Carrots, beets, and radishes are usually seeded directly in the garden. In the Midwest they can be planted in the latter part of April or early in May in rows and about one-half inch deep. Additional plantings at two-week intervals will provide vegetables throughout the summer. The rows must be thinned as the vegetables emerge so that plants will be spaced about two inches apart within each row. Failure to remove excess seedlings will produce poor quality, misshapen root crops. A foot to fourteen inches between rows will provide satisfactory spacing.

Beans cannot be planted until the soil warms up, which means mid-May, at least for midwesterners. Bush-type snap beans mature in sixty days or less and several plantings at two-week intervals will provide fresh beans over a long period. Bean seeds should be planted deeper than most others because they are large. Plant them about two inches deep, six to eight seeds per foot, two feet between rows, and eventually thin them to about three inches between plants. Pick all the beans before the seeds become very large in the pods, and do not leave old pods on the plants or you will reduce the yield considerably.

All of these vegetables, with the exception of tomatoes and peppers, should be harvested while they are young and succulent. Size and color will determine when you should pick peppers and tomatoes.

These vegetables are all easy to grow, but perhaps a bit more information on tomato growing would be helpful. Tomato plants should be planted deeply enough so the lower leaves are just above the soil. If there is a long area of bare stem, you may simply dig a trench and lay the tomato plant on its side. Roots will develop along the buried stem. Of course, the part of the stem with foliage attached to it should not be buried. You can let the stem (really a vine) grow along the ground, but the tomatoes may be attacked by soil microorganisms which destroy them. Some people cover the ground with straw or black plastic to prevent such destruction. The neater way to grow

*Patio-type tomatoes growing in a pot
and fastened to a stake*

*Patio-type tomatoes growing
in a pot on a wire semicircle*

Patio-type cucumbers growing in a pot and encircled by wire

tomatoes, however, is to grow them upright attached to a stake, trellis, or wire cylinder. Easiest of all is to put a five-foot cylinder of concrete reinforcing wire around each tomato plant. The plants will be held upright and won't need pruning. Tomatoes can be picked easily through the large mesh. If you decide to attach the plant to a stake, then side shoots should be removed to limit the plant to one or two main stems. The plants will have to be tied to the stakes. Pruned plants generally produce tomatoes earlier, but unpruned plants will produce tomatoes longer. It's your choice.

Elimination of weeds is a tedious but necessary task. While seedlings are emerging and taking on some size, most weeding will be hand work with the help of a hoe. Later, however, the application of some organic mulch such as peat will keep the soil cooler, smother weeds, and conserve moisture.

Again, plan your garden before planting. The ultimate height of the vegetables will determine their position. Tomatoes should be at the north end of the garden because they will be the tallest if you grow them upright. Beans and peppers are around two feet tall and should be placed to the south of the tomatoes. Cabbage and lettuce plants are short, but taller than the root crops (carrots, beets, and radishes). The size of the garden is limited by your time and ambition, but you will do better to start with a small area, do a good job, and enjoy the yields. If you tackle too big a garden, you will not be happy with the yields, quality, or gardening in general.

*

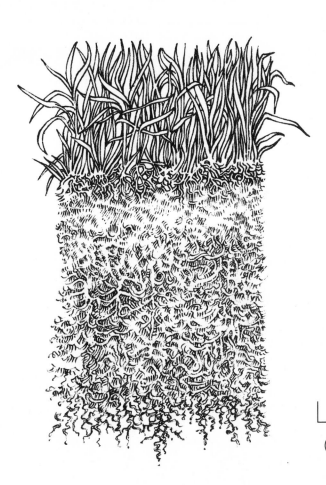

9
LAWNS AND OTHER GROUND COVERS

Lawns are areas on which perennial grasses are established. We will examine some grasses used in lawns around the country and then develop a maintenance program to assist you in producing a top-notch lawn.

First of all, a lawn is really a long-term investment. A lawn may last for hundreds of years. Few gardening achievements bring more satisfaction than a well-maintained lawn that adds much to the beauty of your home. Besides that, the moisture given off each hot summer day by all the foliage has a cooling effect which is best appreciated when an area of equivalent size is transformed into a hot parking lot! A good lawn is the result of the study of lawn grass requirements, planning, preparation, and adherence to a program of good management.

A good lawn grass is perennial, will tolerate mowing, and will respond to reasonable cultural practices, such as watering and fertilizing, by producing a good, uniform cover. Such grasses include Kentucky bluegrass, rough bluegrass, Creeping Red fescue, and various bentgrasses among those having a fine texture (narrow leaf blades). Coarse-bladed grasses having the same characteristics include tall fescue, redtop, timothy, and annual as well as perennial rye. These grasses are all suited for the northern half of the country. Some warm-season grasses suitable for warm, dry climates are St. Augustine, buffalo, centipede, Bermuda, and zoysia.

A lawn may be established by planting grass seed or buying **sod**. Seed will take six weeks to cover an area even under favorable conditions. Sod will do the job in one day—but it is quite expensive. You will have to make the choice. Either method will produce the same results if planted and maintained properly.

We will begin with seed selection. Packages of grass seed vary tremendously in price. There are reasons for this variation that will become apparent if you study the printing on the package. First of all, the package tells you whether fine-textured or coarse-textured grasses are included. Most people consider fine-textured grasses superior in appearance to coarse ones. Coarse blades scattered on a fine-textured lawn look like weeds, such as crab grass or quack. Generally, coarse grasses have much larger seeds than fine grasses. A pound of fine grass may contain ten times as many seeds as a pound of coarse grass.

The name of the grass or grasses also appears on the label, and that will enable you to look up its growth characteristics. An item called "percent germination" is also shown. Obviously no one has tested each package. Large seed lots are tested as they come to the packaging company from the grower. Several samples of a hundred seeds or more are placed in growth chambers where light, temperature, and humidity can be controlled. These seeds are checked after several weeks. The percentage of seeds which have germinated is the figure placed on all packages filled from that seed lot. The higher the germination rate, the more grass you can expect to grow from that package. Figures of 75 percent or higher indicate proper harvesting and storage—and probably more expense. Lower percentage figures mean you are buying seeds that won't grow.

Another figure indicates the percent purity or the amount of material other than grass seed contained in the package. Some of that material may be dirt or chaff; some may be weed seeds or other crop seeds. More expensive seed is thoroughly cleaned and such a package contains 80 percent or more pure grass seed. Cheaper seeds frequently aren't cleaned as well. You then pay for a lot of dirt and chaff.

Since no legal minimums are established, unless you understand the label and resist, you could buy coarse-textured grasses with most of the package filled with dirt, chaff, weeds, and dead grass seeds.

Kentucky bluegrass is the most popular grass for the northern part of the country. Seeds germinate in about three weeks, which is rather slow. Bluegrass requires lots of sunshine and its most serious limitation is its lack of vigor during hot, dry weather. It simply becomes dormant and looks dead (brown). Regular watering will prevent dormancy.

Creeping Red fescue is a more shade-tolerant grass, and it is often mixed with Kentucky bluegrass. Such a mixture will provide fescue for shaded areas and bluegrass will dominate the sunny ones. Red fescue germinates in about half the time required for Kentucky bluegrass.

Tall fescue is a coarse grass used on playgrounds and athletic fields; it cannot be mowed quite as low as the grasses previously mentioned.

Bentgrasses are used for special purposes, such as display areas and golf greens. They also are more susceptible to diseases and require more frequent watering, fertilizing, and mowing. They often suffer from severe winters. But they are beautiful.

Zoysia grows best in hot weather. While it is hardy quite far north, it turns brown with the first frost and remains brown until after the last frost in the spring. That means that in many areas of the Midwest it will be a green lawn only half as long as the other grasses mentioned. It does, however, form a thick sod which squeezes out the weeds, and it is resistant to drought, diseases, and insects.

If you decide to start a new lawn from seeds, your initial investment should not be large. The seed for an average city lot should cost around $30. The time to plant grass seed is during August or early September. The reasons for planting then rather than in the spring have to do with soil temperatures, frost, and day lengths. Both spring and fall generally provide adequate rainfall. In the fall the soil temperature is warm but air temperatures begin to cool off; this favors root development. Springtime has rising air temperatures and soil temperatures, but the soil has been frozen and remains cold quite awhile; this does *not* favor root development. Weeds provide less competition in the fall. Annual weeds will be killed by approaching frosts. Perennial weeds are less apt to germinate with the shorter day lengths in the fall season. So spring is a second choice. Patching small areas can be done at either time.

The preparation of the soil is rather simple. Just clear the area of other vegetation and break up the top one inch of soil—an ordinary rake works well if you have the ambition and the muscle.

Fertilizer should be applied at this time. Lawn fertilizers contain more nitrogen than garden fertilizers because grass plants use it abundantly. The bag should be labeled 20-20-20 or 20-10-10. You can usually rent a fertilizer spreader, which will do a much more even job of spreading the granules than you can do by hand.

The same machine may be used to spread the seed, too. Also available are hand-cranked units. Spread the seed as evenly as possible in the amount indicated on the seed package. The entire area should then be raked again to put some covering over most of the seed.

Some experts advocate spreading a thin layer of straw over this area so that about 75 percent of the ground is covered. This cover will conserve moisture and help in establishing more of the grass plants quickly. A slope where seeds might be washed away should be covered with muslin or burlap through which the grass will grow while the cloth gradually decomposes.

Watering is crucial. While the seeds are germinating and the young plants are becoming established, water is the most important commodity. Daily or twice-daily applications are necessary until you have a green cover over your yard. The volume of water used need not be large, because the seeds are at or near the surface, but the surface does dry out rapidly. A germinating seed that runs out of moisture does not get a second chance; it dies.

Three weeks after seeding, a thick, green growth should be visible. This will not stand foot traffic. Wait another three weeks before allowing any traffic on the lawn.

In direct contrast to seed-established lawns is the ease and convenience of a sod-established lawn. It can be started anytime. But fall is still best, with spring ranking second. Sodding can be finished in a few hours and it may be walked on right away (only regular traffic is discouraged for a week or two). However, the cost may run from $350 to $1,000 for the same size lot that $30 worth of seed would have handled.

Soil preparation is the same as for seed. The sod nursery will bring rolls or rectangular pads of growing grass skimmed from their fields and containing the rhizomes and most of the roots in a thin layer of soil. This is placed on your bare soil, much like carpeting. The cross-seams are alternated and soon disappear. They may press the sod down with a heavy roller to make sure that contact is firm between soil and sod. (This is the only time I would advocate the use of a lawn roller.) Then it is up to you to apply water—lots of water—everyday for the first week, unless it rains. If you are sodding your yard in mid-summer, you will have to continue to water several times each week for a month to overcome the hot, drying sun. During spring and fall, watering the first week is the most important.

Sodding is certainly the more convenient method. It sounds expensive. But it might be worth the difference in cost if you were to be trapped indoors with a number of children while you waited six weeks for seed to become established!

Regardless of the way you start your lawn, the same maintenance program is necessary to keep it in top-notch shape. Fertilizing, watering, mowing, and aerating are the key steps.

Standard lawn fertilizer should be applied twice each year. In the northern half of the country, where cool-season grasses predominate, the heavier fertilization should be given in early September. A light fertilization is given in late March or early April. The fertilizer analysis on the bag will be the same as the one listed earlier: 20-20-20 or 20-10-10. This must be applied evenly or unsightly differences in color will mar the appearance of your lawn, so buy or rent a fertilizer applicator.

An established lawn must have water. Plan to give it the equivalent of one inch of rainful each week. If it rains, you will be spared the effort. But if you don't plan to water each week, you will probably forget to water during weeks when there is no natural rainfall. You can test your sprinkler by placing several straight-sided cans around it and determining how long it takes with the water running to put one inch of water in them. However long that turns out to be is the time you need to run the sprinkler over each area of lawn every week. This watering program will keep the grass green and growing during the hot part of the summer when many of the cool-season grasses become dormant (brown).

A permanently established underground system is a more modern method of watering. You can install this system yourself or have it done for you. Water is distributed through plastic pipes laid rather shallowly under the lawn. At regular intervals pop-up valves reach up above the grass when the water pressure is turned on; they retract beneath the grass blades, safe from the lawn mower, when the water is turned off. Such a system can be regulated by a timing device if you so desire.

Mowing is the one activity in lawn maintenance that most of us have experienced. Mowing frequency depends upon the growth rate of the grass. Mowers should never remove more than one-third of the leaf length at any one time. More severe cutting of the leaves reduces the photosynthetic area too much and endangers the life of the plant. Most lawn grasses are clipped to a height of one and one-half to two inches. This means that we should mow frequently enough so that no more than a half inch is sheared off. In the spring this might mean mowing twice each week. By mid-summer mowing frequency may fall off to once every other week.

The type of mower really doesn't matter so long as the blades are kept sharp. Have the mower put into good condition *before* the mowing season starts.

Clippings should be caught or raked up. A fast-growing lawn needs frequent mowing; if the clippings are allowed to fall among the grass plants, they will cause problems. If they decomposed rapidly, they would be a good source of organic matter for the soil. But they do not! Instead, clippings accumulate during spring and fall when rapid growth occurs and eventually form an almost impermeable layer, called **thatch**. Thatch may actually prevent water and air from penetrating into the soil around the roots. When that happens, growth stops. The grass plants may die. Even when the clippings are caught or raked up, many of them escape and fall to the ground; they will provide enough organic matter.

The last of the regularly scheduled steps in lawn maintenance is aerating. This may be done either in spring or fall. The point of aerating is to try to relieve compaction and eliminate thatch, thus allowing air and water easy access to the soil. Power rakes may be rented to accomplish this; or you may rent an aerator which you push around while teeth on its wheels punch holes in the lawn. Other machines actually pull plugs out of the soil. Of course, you can also use a heavy steel-toothed rake and "muscle" it around the lawn. Aerating means deeper raking than the cosmetic raking that is done to pick up leaves in the fall. This step is actually a rather new process introduced into maintenance programs in recent years. It has turned out to be a very good addition. Your lawn will benefit.

Weed control may be achieved with chemicals or through biological means. Broad-leaved plants which appear in your lawn, such as dandelions, are rather unsightly. I suppose we would admire and cultivate them if they were difficult to grow. But they grow and increase in numbers so easily that they become a nuisance. The biological control is you! Dig them out! A kitchen knife makes a handy tool for this job, and you can enjoy an afternoon in the sun digging weeds. Should you decide that is too time-consuming, chemicals aplenty exist to eliminate the broad-leaved weeds. Best known of these chemicals is 2, 4–D. If you spray your yard in the fall, the following summer you will have few weeds problems. A wax bar impregnated with 2,4–D may be simply drawn along while you walk around the yard. This bar eliminates drift problems that may occur by using chemicals in liquid sprays. Another easily used instrument is a tube that is punched down on each of the weeds. You fill the tube with water and add the chemical, which comes in the form of a wafer. This restricts the chemical to a single plant.

Problems caused by insects and disease organisms are best left to experts. Your county or state extension agents can probably advise you on the steps necessary for solving those problems. Such problems are rare, however. I really don't foresee any such difficulties for the average lawn.

So far we have been discussing a ground cover. Ground covers are materials used to protect soil from erosion by wind or rain and at the same time improve the appearance of that area. Grass is the most common ground cover used in the Midwest.

But grass has limitations. It does not grow well in the shade. It is difficult to establish on steep slopes. It usually is not planted in rocky areas or where the surface is very irregular, because it cannot be mowed under those conditions. Grass will stand quite a bit of foot traffic, but cannot endure where a regular, heavy traffic pattern occurs. (In other words, a path of dead grass will form.) Where any of these situations prevail, some material other than grass will have to be used.

Ground covers do not have to be living plants. A wide variety of inorganic (or at least nonliving) materials may be used. And I think many of them would provide a pleasing contrast in your yard. With a green lawn, green garden plants, and green shrubs, it doesn't hurt to inject some other color to break the monotony. A graveled path or brick patio can be a pleasant contrast to the dominant green. Certainly areas which receive heavy, constant traffic will need covering with some nonliving ground cover. Wooden blocks, large stones, sand or gravel held by cement or some of the newer epoxy-type glues, marble chips or limestone chips or wood chips, and even concrete, which may be colored to suit you, can be used attractively.

There may be areas which do not receive much traffic and in which grass cannot be grown. The following plants are easy to grow and able to survive over most of the country. For places in your yard that receive direct sunlight most of the day, but which may be rocky or uneven or steeply sloped, try creeping phlox, which I have described earlier. Several species of *Sedum* will work well, too. One called gold cup moss is very short, like a carpet, and has yellow flowers. Delightful. To cover an embankment try junipers. The horizontal, or prostrate forms of this shrub are frequently used in such a location. They can be planted five feet apart and will eventually blanket the area with their ground-hugging branches.

For shady areas any of the following plants will do: lily-of-the-valley, hosta, periwinkle (*Vinca minor*), and several euonymus varieties which are woody vines.

Skillful use of ground cover materials can certainly improve the appearance and value of your property.

GLOSSARY

Sod: The soil surface and a short distance beneath which has become a mat of intertwining grass roots.

Thatch: A layer of grass clippings in the lawn which may become thick and matted enough to interfere with growth of the grass.

10

TREES AND SHRUBS

In our examination of trees we will look first at the mechanics of handling them from purchase through planting and beyond; then we will look at the ways you may use trees in designing a home landscape.

The least expensive type of tree to purchase is one called a bare root tree. This is a young tree with a small root system and no soil around the roots so it may be sent through the mail. That, plus the fact it did not need to be grown for a very long time in the nursery, makes it an inexpensive plant. Bare root trees are usually sold through mail order catalogs. These young trees, which may have been started from seed, grafting, or cuttings, are planted close together in rows in the nursery fields. They may grow there for only one year or as long as five depending on the type of tree. They are dug in the fall when they have reached salable size. After being dug rather roughly by machine and trucked into a storage building, they are stacked in cool rooms and their roots covered with peat or wood shavings. This covering is kept moist to prevent dehydration of the roots. When you send an order to the nursery for one of these trees, the shipper waits until the proper time in the spring for planting in your area, pulls a tree from the pile, prunes broken roots or branches, and wraps the roots in moss and plastic and the entire tree in heavy paper. The tree is then mailed to you. Since the size of the tree is limited by postal regulations, you might be disappointed if you looked at catalog pictures of a mature tree fifty feet tall and thirty feet wide when in full leaf and then receive a four-foot tree with a few short branches and bare roots. But, if properly cared for, that little stick will become a tree like the one pictured. Begin by soaking the roots in a bucket of water for a day or two before planting. Then dig a straight-sided hole a foot deeper and a foot wider than the root system, put a cone of soil at the bottom of this hole and use it as a base to support the stem of the tree. When the tree is in place, spread the roots around the cone of soil. Fill the hole about one-third full of soil and pour in some water; then fill it another one-third and add more water. Finally, finish filling the hole but leave a saucer-shaped depression around the stem. The depression allows runoff water from surrounding soil to accumulate around the root system. When first planted, all the roots will be just beneath the stem, and the tree can use all the water it can get. The tree should be planted at the same depth it was growing in the nursery, or possibly one inch deeper. You can tell how deep it was previously planted by the color change along the base of the stem.

Balled and burlapped
evergreen shrub

You might, however, decide to buy a tree from your local nursery. This will be a larger, well-established tree, which will give you immediate benefits. It will have been pruned, fertilized, and protected for a number of years, so it will cost you quite a bit more than the bare root tree. This tree will arrive at your home in the condition called **balled and burlapped**—or some modification of it. Generally the nurseryman digs around the existing root system and encloses the roots, with their attendant soil ball, in burlap. This heavy, awkward tree with soil is lifted onto a truck and delivered to your home, where a hole big enough to accommodate the soil ball is dug. The tree is then dropped into the hole with the burlap still around the roots (burlap will soon decompose and does not interfere with root growth). The only necessary precaution is to make sure no wires, nails, or clips still hold the burlap around the stem or trunk of the tree. A tree like this still has most of its roots and they are functioning, although there is some loss of roots from digging. It therefore has a much better chance for life than the bare root tree—and nurseries will guarantee their trees.

A modification of this system has come about since the invention of several machines capable of digging trees. The machine is used to dig a hole in your yard first, or a hole is dug by hand. Then the machine is placed around a tree and its blades dig a soil ball surrounding the root system and lift the entire mass. Still held in the machine, the tree is then driven to the planting site and dropped into the hole. No burlap is used because the steel blades surround the soil ball. Would you call that "balled and steeled"? At any rate, it is a soil ball system, and trees up to twelve inches in diameter may be moved successfully this way. Many evergreen shrubs and trees of large dimensions are handled in this manner. Obviously this kind of handling will add to the cost.

Container-grown plants are the nursery equivalent to the pot plants of the florists' trade. Young trees are planted in large containers made of metal, plastic, wood pulp, or other sturdy material and are grown in those containers until sold. Since these trees cannot be tended by driving a tractor along the rows to spread fertilizer, and they are above ground and ex-

posed to air movement (drying) and extremes of temperature (winter kill), special watering and fertilizing
systems have been devised to prevent dehydration.
Mulches must be used to insulate the containers. But
plants may be crowded together at first and spaced as
they grow, the root system remains intact and needs
no pruning to develop compactly, and the trees are
easily handled and moved.

Container-grown evergreen shrub

Planting a container-grown tree may be done any
time. The container must be removed first, but the
ground hole need be only as large as the container.
Little transplanting shock occurs. Such plants are too
heavy for individual shipment, so they are usually
trucked to a retail outlet and sold locally. Expense of
growing such a plant is greater for a given time length
than for either of the other two methods of growing.

Convenience in handling and assurance of continued life are the factors that make this method increasingly popular.

Young and newly planted trees need lots of water. Of course they should be given a thorough soaking immediately following planting. During the first growing season, they should be watered once each week, receiving the equivalent of about one inch of rainfall. If it rains that much, naturally the watering may be skipped that week.

The next step is the matter of bracing a tree. Suppose you planted a bare root tree in the spring. It has a very limited root system. As leaves develop on the upper part of the plant, they present some wind resistance, with the result that when strong winds blow, the tree rocks back and forth in the soil. This rocking action will tear off root hairs and damage young tender roots that are being formed. Growth is slowed or stopped. The tree itself may end up tipped at an angle. Even trees which were container grown or balled and burlapped are subject to that wind action although to a lesser extent. The way to prevent this disaster is to brace the tree when you plant it.

Methods for staking trees

Methods for staking trees

*Methods for staking trees;
note wrapping*

Small trees (up to eight feet) may be adequately supported with a metal fence post driven into the ground six to twelve inches away from the trunk on the side from which the prevailing summer winds blow. The tree is then fastened to the stake. Care must be taken, however, to prevent damage to the tree trunk. Wire or rope will eventually saw through the bark and may kill the tree. Broad strips of plastic or rubber hose are placed around the tree, and then wire is run through the hose and twisted around the stake. The nonabrasive surface of the hose will protect the tree bark while still holding the tree securely and almost permanently by the enclosed wire. Should the tree be too tall to receive support from a fence post, wires or cables may be attached to the tree by the above method and run to stakes driven into the ground. Three or four such wires run in different directions will give excellent support.

Pruning of some branches will be necessary on all but container-grown trees because some damage has been done to the root systems when digging either bare root or balled and burlapped trees. With bare root trees, for example, we know they were dug and handled roughly—that was part of the economy. Some roots were lost. The tops and branches, however, are usually intact. If leaves emerge on the upper part of the complete top of such a tree, the reduced root system will not be able to supply sufficient water for them; the result is wilting, loss of leaves, and possibly the death of the tree. To compensate for the root loss, we estimate that one-third of the root system has been lost and balance that loss by cutting back each branch by one-third. *Do not* cut back the main stem or trunk unless you want a permanently shortened tree. A balled and burlapped tree which has had proper nursery care should not need a pruning that severe, but it will need some.

Every newly planted tree needs protection from rodents, and most need protection from the sun. A wire cylinder made of hardware cloth and extending up-ward from the ground at least three feet will give protection against foraging by mice, rabbits, and go-phers during the winter when other foot is scarce. If your area receives much snow, the cylinder must reach high enough so a rabbit cannot stand on top of the snow and stretch above the wire to chew the bark off your tree. This is only necessary during the win-ter. Similar protection may be provided by wrapping the trunk of the tree with a heavy paper sold by garden centers. The paper should be spiraled up the trunk from the ground to the lowest branch and left on until it deteriorates. You could use aluminum foil for a wrapping. It will work as well but looks a bit gaudy in your yard. Wrapping also provides protec-tion from the sun. Sun scald is overheating of the bark on the south side of the tree that occurs because the tree now has little or no winter shade. In the nursery it was surrounded by other trees. Even in the winter bare tree branches provided passing shade from the sun. Now the tree is alone in your yard with its branches pruned back and no leaves to help shade it. Long exposure to the sun may kill patches of bark; these dead areas crack and eventually disease organ-isms or insects may enter the tree through them. Even if they don't, the bark falls off and leaves scars on the tree trunk. Some types of trees are more easily damaged than others.

Fertilizer should be applied to trees during the spring after growth has started. For a young tree this means placing the granular material at the base of the trunk because all the roots are compactly centered beneath that area. But as the tree grows with age, the roots extend too. An old tree will have roots extended even farther than the spread of its branches. The old roots, which are directly under the tree trunk, no longer absorb water and minerals to any appreciable degree. The roots performing this function are the new, young roots at the periphery of the root system.

That is where you must apply fertilizer. A good guess is that this active root area is approximately beneath the tips of the outermost branches—the "drip line." These roots, however, are several feet beneath the soil. Were you to place the fertilizer on the ground at that point, only the grass would benefit; you must get the fertilizer down near the roots. In the past, holes were formed by driving a piece of pipe into the ground at intervals of a few feet around the entire drip line, then fertilizer was washed down each hole. Today instruments called root feeders, which can be attached to a garden hose, are available at your garden center. Fertilizer in stick form is placed in the tool. After the hose has been attached and the water turned on, the tool is plunged into the ground at intervals. The water dissolves the solid fertilizer and washes it down the tube into the ground. This puts the fertilizer below the grass roots, making it available to the tree. An old tree will benefit from yearly applications of fertilizer as much as a young tree.

Root feeder

A tree is a long-term investment and should be carefully selected. Mostly it's a matter of understanding why you are buying a tree. Perhaps the environmental effects concern you. An apple tree in your backyard gives off enough oxygen in a year to supply four people. It (or any comparable tree) has a cooling effect, through transpiration, of about ten room air conditioners running most of the day. Of course, an apple tree can also supply you with fruit, shade, privacy, and wind protection. Its flowers, form, foliage color, and twig shapes are esthetically pleasing. One tree can provide all this.

Before deciding what to plant, you must also consider where to plant. We can lump trees into groups according to their ultimate size. Trees fifty feet or taller generally look best in the backyard where they serve as "background" trees, providing a leafy canopy against which to view the house from the front. In a sense, such trees provide an upper frame for a picture of your home. Sometimes you can use trees whose outlines complement the architectural style of the house. A few such trees are maples (round, oval), sycamore (round), cottonwood (spreading), oaks (oval, spreading, pyramidal), hackberry (vase), and American linden (oval).

A second size category includes medium-sized trees, twenty-five to fifty feet tall. These we can label "framing" trees. They are usually planted to frame the sides of the house—once again, a picture frame. They must be selected with your house in mind. Too tall a framing tree will dwarf your home. A big two- or three-story house can use a fifty-foot framing tree, but not a one-story ranch style home. Some trees in this group are conifers (columnar, pyramidal), little leaf linden (oval), horse chestnut (oval), poplar (columnar), Russian olive (spreading), hawthorn (round), Ohio buckeye (oval), and locust (spreading).

The third group consists of small trees, less than twenty-five feet tall, which we call "display" trees. These trees are usually chosen for the beauty of their foliage or flowers and are planted wherever you wish an accent point. Consider them as you would any other garden perennial so far as placement is concerned. These small trees add a new dimension to shrub borders. They also break the dull horizontal line formed by the top of a fence. A few are Amur maple (oval), cherries (spreading, oval), plums (oval), crabapples (oval, columnar, weeping), mountain ash (oval), service berry (oval), and red bud (spreading).

A few precautions should be taken to save you headaches later. Do not plant trees directly under power lines or telephone wires, for they will ultimately be given a severe pruning to keep them from touching the wires. This type of pruning destroys their shape and beauty. The trees in the "display" category may be planted as close as ten feet to the house or other buildings, but larger trees should be kept at least fifteen feet away. Sidewalks, driveways, and patios may be disrupted by roots if any, but very small trees are planted closer than ten feet. And do not crowd trees together. If crowded, none of the trees will assume its natural shape. Forty to sixty feet from trunk to trunk is necessary for large and medium-sized trees, so keep the eventual spread of each tree in mind when planting them in groups or rows.

Shrubs, like trees, may be purchased as bare root, balled and burlapped, or container-grown plants. The techniques for handling them are the same as for trees, except that bracing and wrapping are not necessary. Bracing can be eliminated because a young shrub simply is not top-heavy enough to rock in the soil. Because shrubs have a number of stems instead of just one, sunburn does not occur, or if it does, at least the entire plant is not endangered. Protection against rodents is optional. Rodents may chew off an entire hedge even of old plants. But new stems will arise from the stubs of old ones so the plant will not be destroyed. A tree has only one trunk, and if that is killed, you are better off getting a new tree than trying to nurse a new shoot to tree proportions.

Placement of shrubs, like placement of trees, needs to be well planned. We shall look at several ways to use shrubs for effective landscaping.

Two or more shrubs placed together are called a "group" planting. Such group plantings are used to tie the house in with its surroundings by eliminating the "box on flat ground" appearance and making the house look like it belongs there. Group plantings are most effective at the corners, near doorways, and along the foundations of a house. Generally some or all of these shrubs are evergreen so their effect is not lost in winter. In sunny locations some spreading type of juniper is often used. Where there is little sun, the most popular evergreen shrub is the yew. Please notice that upright, columnar, or pyramidal trees like spruce, fir, and pine should *not* be used here. Group plantings of evergreen or deciduous shrubs make interesting accent points along a wall, fence, or patio.

A second use for shrubs is as a **border mass**. In fact, small trees might be included with these shrubs in some situations. A border mass is a large number of plants used to define a border or boundary or to obstruct traffic, vision, wind, or snow. Sometimes border shrubs are pruned each year to form a stiff, rather formal row. These plants must be placed quite close together (twelve to fifteen inches). Such formality, however, is not common in modern gardens. More often shrubs used as a border mass are placed at distances which allow them to assume their natural shapes. Plant border masses to mark off various areas in your yard or as a background for a flower border. Staggering several kinds of shrubs of different heights to form a rather wide mass presents foliage interestingly and adds privacy to the yard. Alpine current and barberry are both low shrubs which grow to about three feet. Spirea, privet, and euonymus are medium-sized shrubs from three to six feet tall. Tall shrubs such as lilac and honeysuckle will eventually reach six to ten feet high.

One more way to use shrubs is for "display"—for their beauty alone. Plant such shrubs just as you would any garden perennial. For beautiful flowers you might choose mock orange, flowering quince, flowering almond, forsythia, or the ever popular rose. Two shrubs that have lovely foliage are the red-leaved plum and feathery tamarisk. The bright-colored twigs

An example of topiary: an evergreen (juniper) pruned to an unusual shape

of dogwood are attractive all year round. And, of course, display shrubs may also be part of a group planting or border mass.

An espaliered pear tree

GLOSSARY

Balled and burlapped: Trees or shrubs that have been dug with a large amount of soil surrounding their roots. This soil is kept in place by wrapping it with burlap or some other material.

Border mass: A large number of shrubs planted in a row to define a border or obstruct traffic, vision, wind, or snow.

Espalier: Trees which have been pruned to grow in a single plane.

Topiary: Trees or shrubs which have been pruned to resemble unusual shapes.

11

PEST CONTROL

All plants are subject to damage from some diseases or insect enemies. During certain summers these may be more prevalent than usual. You may go for years with little or no loss of garden plants and then "whap" —you lose a bunch. About some things, like Dutch elm disease, there is little you can do. But there are a number of things you can do about the more common plant problems. It would be impossible here to deal with every plant pest, but I shall mention some general problems you should recognize and be able to control.

First, it will be helpful to understand a little about the more common plant diseases caused by microorganisms called **fungi**. **Mildew** is such a disease which looks like a white or gray mold on the upper surface of leaves. Sometime during the summer you will find it on the foliage of roses, lilacs, zinnias, and possibly apple or pear trees. Mildew dehydrates the leaves and interferes with photosynthesis by reducing the light that reaches the leaf surface. **Botrytis** is a disease which may occur on any part of the plant. The organism responsible enters the plant through some injured area and causes tan to brown spots which enlarge and eventually appear to rot. Often a gray to tan mold will become visible over the infected area. "Scab" and "rust" will be found on apple or pear trees; both leaves and fruit may become infected. Brown or yellow spots occur on the foliage and these enlarge or even coalesce. On the fruit the spots become sunken areas producing deformed fruit.

Insects produce a wide variety of symptoms but most are easy to identify. Large insects may chew irregular holes in the leaf or along leaf edges. Some large insects roll the leaf into a tight cylinder. These insects are easy to spot and can be removed by hand, or in severe infestations, controlled with chemical sprays. Incidentally, the surest insect control known has been jokingly labeled the "hammer and anvil" method—put the insect on an anvil and hit it with a hammer; complete control of that insect results. Hand picking of insects is in that category: slow but sure.

Small insects are more difficult to control. They do not produce visible holes on the leaves so they do considerable damage before symptoms are evident. Most of them are sucking insects that insert a tiny stylet through the surface and suck out the cell sap. The leaves will appear to dry up. At first they become a pale green, then yellow, finally brown. Red spiders (really mites) occur on evergreens and on the underside of the leaves on roses, phlox, and many other ornamental plants. With a hand lens you can spot these mites running around on the lower side of the leaves. Aphids, however, are visible to the naked eye. They attack the young, succulent shoots on any plants, remove the liquid from the inside of the new shoot, and leave it hanging limp. Scale insects are so named because they have a shell like a fish scale with which they attach themselves to plant leaves and stems. They may be brown or white. Scale insects are found on evergreens, ferns, and many houseplants whose origin was a florist's greenhouse, and they must be pried up or chemically controlled.

You can try to control plant pests in several ways. First, purchase plant varieties resistant or immune to a particular pest which afflicts most varieties. This requires a bit of reading between the lines in catalogs or a direct recommendation from some authority, such as your extension agent. In a catalog where many varieties of a particular flower or tree might be described, one of them may mention that a certain variety is resistant to a disease. Descriptions of the other varieties will not say they are susceptible. This you will have to infer. Buy the resistant variety; chances are the other varieties have a severe problem with that disease.

Second, you should buy plant materials, particularly the more expensive nursery stock such as trees and shrubs, from reputable dealers, people who plan to remain in business for years to come. These people want your future business and will sell you disease-free and insect-free plant material. This way you will be more likely to start with healthy plants.

All of the procedures we discussed earlier for starting and maintaining gardens, such as preparation of a well-drained bed, fertilizing, watering, and cultivating, are additional aids to overcoming pests. Not that producing healthy plants will prevent disease or insect attack. It will not! But healthy, vigorous plants may survive such attacks and still produce flowers or fruit. Weed eradication in and *around* your garden is another means of reducing potential pest attacks. Insects move from weeds to your garden plants. Frequently disease organisms live in the weeds without harming them but are carried by insects to your garden plants where they do cause damage. Elimination of the weeds reduces the possibility of pest damage.

Another defense is the use of biological controls. This means introducing some living organism that preys upon another organism which is a plant pest. An example would be the introduction of the praying mantis, an insect, into your garden to help reduce the aphid population. The mantis is a long, thin insect aptly nicknamed the "walking stick." Egg cases of such insects may be purchased through advertisements in garden magazines. Egg cases containing several hundred eggs are placed in the garden in the early summer; they hatch and release this new insect that eats aphids and other pesty insects. The mantis will not kill *all* the aphids but may reduce the population below the number which will do extensive harm to your garden. Ladybugs perform the same way. Obviously, no chemical pesticides can be used without also harming the biological control, and several problems may occur that reduce the effectiveness of biological controls. One problem with the praying mantis is our inability to confine it to a specific area. If your garden cannot provide enough aphids, the mantis will move down the block looking for a bigger food supply. Or one mantis may simply eat another and another until the control force becomes too small to do any good.

Another type of biological control involves plants. Onions, garlic, chives, and marigolds are interspersed between other flowers or vegetables because they repel some insect pests. On the other hand, dill and zinnias may be planted as "trap crops"—some insects are so drawn to them that they feed exclusively on those plants and leave the others alone.

Two problems have been encountered with biological controls. One is that the introduced organism sometimes becomes a worse pest than the one it was supposed to control. To prevent that, a long testing period through many seasonal and annual variations in weather conditions and pest populations is necessary. The second problem is that many biological controls are aimed at one or two major pests but thousands exist. We have not yet found broad biological controls for our many problems nor have we specific controls for each of the many pests. But research is continuing toward these goals.

More recently insect sex attractants have been synthesized and used in fields to draw male insects into traps. Not only are the males trapped, but they do not mate with females, and the total population is greatly reduced. Such chemicals are limited in scope, however, because they only attract one species of insect. This seems now like a great new, nonpolluting chemical system for insect control; it may be the control system of the future.

For the present, however, we are still dependent upon chemical **insecticides** and **fungicides** for protection from the majority of plant pests. In the past there have been many abuses of the environment with excessive use of chemicals or misuse of dangerous chemicals. These are being corrected and controlled. Notice that I have not mentioned "ecology." That term has become so misused and misunderstood that it is almost worthless. When you plant a garden, you disturb the ecology. Pulling the weeds from your garden further upsets the ecology. Is that bad?

The most commonly used method for pest protection is to buy an "all purpose" chemical, a combination of fungicides and insecticides. This chemical may be applied as a dust or powder if it has been prepared for that use by combination with some inert carrier. More often it must be combined with water in the proportions indicated on the package. This mixture is then sprayed over all the exposed plant tissues. The type of instrument will depend upon the number of plants you wish to protect. Liquid sprays probably give more uniform coverage and last longer on the plant than do the dusts or powders. However, the dusts are frequently sold in an applicator, eliminating mixing and cleaning and the additional purchase of an applicator. The sprays will need to be applied every ten to fourteen days all during the growing season if newly formed tissues are to be completely protected from pests. Dusts are easily blown away, so they need to be applied at intervals of seven to ten days. Either type of chemical will be washed off by rain, necessitating its reapplication. When using chemicals *read the labels*! Follow the directions closely and *thoroughly* clean the applicator after each use.

The all-purpose chemical system should give you complete protection from pests. But it means much work and using a lot of chemicals. My own system has been to simply wait until I observe some symptoms of insect or disease damage in the garden and then apply the chemicals. Two or three applications in a two-week period will probably eliminate the problem. I recognize that using this system I may lose some plants or reduce the yield of vegetables, flowers, or fruit. On the other hand, many years I do not have to use any chemicals. So long as I am not engaged in plant production as a commercial venture, a small loss is easily acceptable.

Control of pests on houseplants is easier. If you keep the foliage dry and follow the suggestions on watering given earlier, diseases are not likely to be a problem. But insects may build up in numbers. Any-

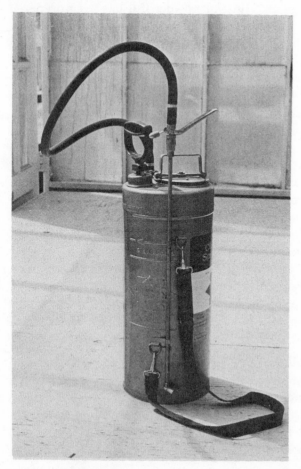

Large sprayer for garden pesticide application

time you take houseplants outdoors during the summer or bring home a new houseplant, you may introduce some insect pests. Again, the large ones are easily seen and picked off. Even scale insects can be removed with your fingernails. A cotton swab dipped in alcohol may be touched to aphids and scale insects to kill them. Normal cleaning of houseplant foliage will remove most of the sucking insects. Should the problem persist, however, you have two courses of action available. The cheapest is to buy an insecticide chemical, mix it in a bucket, put on rubber gloves, and dip the infested foliage in the liquid. This method is very effective but a lot of work. More expensive, but simpler, is the purchase of an aerosol can containing pesticides. So long as only a few plants are involved this works well. It is also a method that can be used to eliminate insects which sometimes invade a terrarium. The fog produced by the aerosol makes a nice film over exposed plant tissues.

Four types of applicators for pest control

Oddly, some people never seem to have pest problems while others are constantly plagued. I think luck and perhaps overzealousness both enter in here. In any case, do the best you can, but if a plant dies, don't grieve. It is not a person or a pet. Plants are not irreplaceable. Learn what you can from the experience and *buy another plant*! That is the beauty of growing plants.

GLOSSARY

Botrytis: A disease of plants caused by fungi.

Fungi: A class of plants which lacks chlorophyll and obtains sustenance by living on other plants or animals.

Fungicide: A chemical that will destroy a fungus or several kinds of fungi.

Insecticide: A chemical that will destroy an insect or several types of insects.

Mildew: A disease of plants caused by fungi.

12

LANDSCAPING

Planting trees, shrubs, and flowers without first forming an overall design will not produce a pleasing landscape—just a plant collection. Planning comes before planting. Landscaping means to make the best use of available space in the most attractive way. Even if you buy an older home which has been landscaped (or at least planted), it is a good idea to develop your own plan and then gradually make your plantings conform to it.

First, you need to recognize the activities of greatest importance to you and your family. If sports are a primary interest, then perhaps a swimming pool or badminton court will be a prominent part of your landscape design. Or gardening, either flower or vegetable, may be your consuming interest and should be included in the design. Perhaps you will use your backyard for entertaining guests. This calls for another type of design. You may also wish to have a children's play area. Any of these can be worked in so long as you plan ahead for them.

You also need to recognize and plan around good and bad features already existing on or near your property. Trees or shrubs or wild flowers presently growing there may be incorporated into your landscape. If you can see a hill or a lake in the distance, you might be able to frame that scene with trees or shrubs and visually include it as part of your yard. A park or golf course nearby could also become part of your yard if you landscape properly.

On the other hand, if your neighbor collects old cars or tires, you certainly want to screen off that view. A house poorly oriented on the lot might have its appearance improved with compensating plants. Neighbors' picture windows may face your yard and your "goldfish" feeling will have to be soothed with screening that provides privacy.

With these basic needs established the drawing can begin with a scale plan of the house and property. On the plan you need to indicate the distance from the street to the front of the house, slopes, power lines, existing plantings, window and door openings, service and living areas in the house, driveway, sidewalk, and so forth. Tracing paper or plastic overlays should then be placed over this scale drawing and the designing begins.

A good landscape design will include three major areas: service, public, and private. We shall examine each of these at some length.

The service area should be adjacent to the kitchen, back door, basement entrance, utility room, garage, and any other part of your home considered a physical work area. Usually, in any good architectural plan, these areas are designed to be close to one another. You will need this outdoor service area for trash cans, incinerator, clothesline, storage shed, dog house, or other equipment peculiar to your household. This is, generally speaking, an unsightly area. It is also an area used year around. Therefore, it should be surfaced with some material which you will not track into the house; cement, cement block, flagstone, gravel, asphalt, brick, and wood block are some available surfacing materials. Because it is an area which is not attractive, it should be screened off from the street, your own backyard, and probably the neighbor's yard. The screening may be accomplished with fencing or shrubbery, but be sure to leave entryways from several directions so the area is readily accessible. If you choose not to screen it on the neighbor's side, he may do it anyway! Who wants to look at garbage cans?

The public area is that part of your yard seen from the street. We are limited here to a rather simple plan. If your front yard flows smoothly into the next yard, it has the effect of doubling your lot size. In addition, an uncluttered yard will appear to have more depth than one broken up with plantings. For most of us it will be beneficial to have the house appear farther back from the street than it really is.

Three things should be accomplished in the public area: to soften the architectural lines of the building, to draw attention to the front door, and to frame the building.

The reason a new house often looks so stark is that its strong vertical lines contrast so sharply with the horizontal line of the ground. If you can somehow soften that contrast, the house will seem to be more a part of the landscape. A group planting of shrubs placed at the corners of the house may accomplish this. Using rounded or spreading shrubs of different heights in combination at each corner will have the visual effect of making a smooth transition from the vertical to the horizontal. The ultimate height of this corner planting should not exceed two-thirds of the distance from the ground to the eaves. With two-story houses a small tree could be part of this group planting. You can lower the apparent height of the house by extending this group planting farther to the side, away from the house. Such an extended "wing" to a corner planting will also provide a screen between the street and the backyard.

In addition to the concave line such a planting forms leading to the ground, it also forms a similar line leading toward the front door. This is a subtle means of drawing attention to the front door. A more obvious way is to group plantings at either side of the front door. These shrubs will also soften the sharp vertical lines of the door. Should the doorway happen to be off to one side rather than in the center, this doorway planting may be used to visually balance the house. By putting a taller group of shrubs on the short side of the house, it will appear "heavier" to the eye and compensate for the longer wall and lower shrubs on the other side of the door. You can estimate the proper height for doorway plantings by drawing a line from the top of the corner planting (two-thirds the height between ground and eaves) to a spot at the bottom center of the front door. This line will indicate the maximum height of the doorway plantings. As with corner plantings, use only spreading or rounded shrubs.

The previous two types of group plantings will still leave some areas of the house bare of plants. That's fine. There is no reason to put shrubbery over the entire front of the house. In fact, doing so tends to shorten the house, for you really only substitute the green line of the shrubs for the green line of the lawn. You may wish to put a group planting along the foundation just for interest, something to break the monotony of a blank wall. Or perhaps you have a bare, unattractive foundation showing and wish to cover it. These plantings are called foundation plantings and are another form of group planting.

The three types of group plantings just discussed are usually made up of evergreen shrubs, for we want the effect to last all year long. Deciduous shrubs may be added to each group, but the majority should be evergreen.

The most popular evergreen shrubs are the many species and varieties of juniper. Their growth habits range from prostrate, through spreading, to pyramidal. (Pyramidal types should *not* be planted near the house). These are all sun-loving shrubs. So is the mugho pine, another evergreen shrub, which does not seem to be as popular as it once was. For shaded areas, even areas that never receive any sun, the yew (*Taxus*), which has several different forms, is by far the most popular.

Framing the house is achieved with trees and lawn. The broad, unbroken expanse of lawn should provide a lower frame for the picture of your house. You may have a driveway cutting through the lawn, but in our car-oriented society not much can be done about that.

However, you should *not* emphasize the driveway with plants. Plantings of shrubs or flowers just make the driveway more obvious, and they may become a safety hazard. Any further segmenting of the lawn can be avoided, however, by using the driveway as a walk and simply running a short sidewalk from the door to the driveway, parallel to the house. From the street this will seem to be part of the foundation and will not contribute to the checkerboard effect so frequently seen in front yards where a series of intersections between sidewalks and driveways occur.

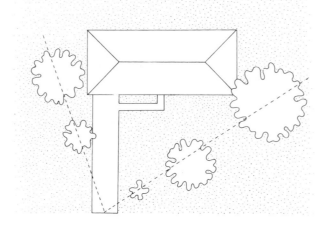

Framing trees

The upper frame for this picture you are creating will be, hopefully, the canopy formed by background trees. Lacking that, you will have to settle for blue sky until you can grow such trees.

The side frames will be formed by medium-sized trees properly placed. There is no one correct way to place such framing trees; the possibilities are numerous. Start by picking some point along the street from where you think most people will view your home. This might be the center of the lot or the foot of the driveway or some other place. Working from your scale plan, draw a line from this point past one corner of the front of the house, passing the line roughly eight to ten feet from the structure. Somewhere along that line you should plant a tree to be the frame for that side of your house. Exact placement along the line is your option; you may want to plant the tree where it will shade a bedroom or hide a jog in the roof. You need also keep in mind that the nearer to the street you plant this tree, the smaller (ultimate height) tree you should select. This, of course, has to do with scale. You must select a tree that will neither dwarf your home nor make it appear too large. The nearness to the street will alter its apparent size. Tree shape should also be a consideration. If you have a one-story ranch-style house which spreads out along the landscape, a spreading tree would complement the house shape. Gabled homes can use trees with sharper, pyramidal outlines.

Having determined where one framing tree will be planted, repeat the process for the other side of the house. As a general rule, the second tree should not be in the same plane as the first. Or, to put it another way, the second tree should not be the same distance from the street as the first. Trees planted in the same plane create a rather stilted and formal appearance.

Because roots and branches continue to lengthen, be careful not to plant framing trees closer to the house than fifteen or twenty feet. Display trees may be planted closer, but even they should be no closer than eight or ten feet. It is also wise to keep trees at least ten feet from driveways or sidewalks. And, finally, avoid planting trees in front of windows and doors unless the view from them is objectionable.

The private or living area, your backyard, should reflect your interests. That is about the only rule for planning that applies, but try to make the view from within the living area of your house as pleasant as you

can. Screen unpleasant views with shrubs or fencing.
Then, standing in the yard, you must determine what
can be done to improve appearances. Privacy is usually a prerequisite. This can be achieved with border
mass plantings or fencing or a combination of the two.
If gardening is your hobby and you have the time for
it, then large garden areas may be planned. Or a
small garden placed at the back of the yard may serve
as a focal point of your design. A birdbath or feeder
might be a focal point if bird-watching is your hobby.

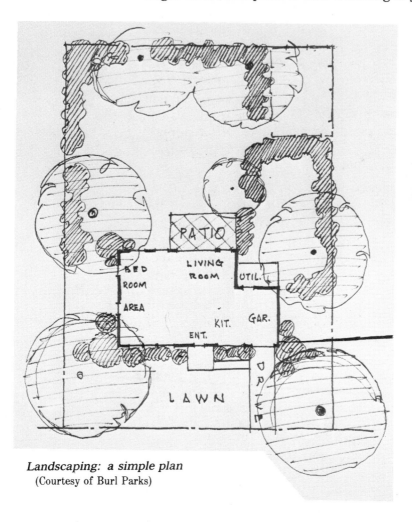

Landscaping: a simple plan
(Courtesy of Burl Parks)

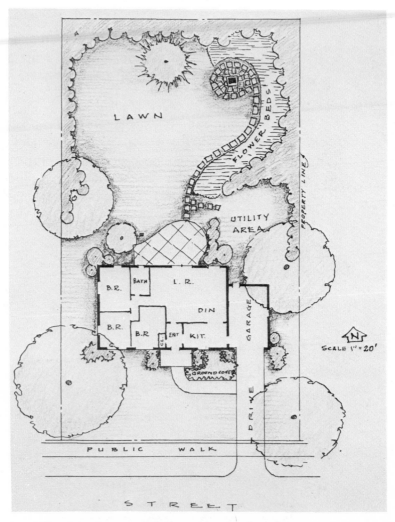

Landscaping: a modern, more complex plan
(Courtesy of Burl Parks)

The basic design could be formal with equal plantings on either side of the yard and straight lines and right angles dominating. But asymmetrical designs with curving lines are more natural and informal; this seems to be the trend today. The simplest example would be a broad, sweeping curve around the entire backyard with shrubs planted singly in the narrow areas along the property lines and combinations of shrubs filling out the wider portions. A judicious choice of shrubs might provide color at various times during the growing season and still give you a very easily maintained yard.

The construction of a raised area will make the yard immeasurably more interesting. Just elevating a small bed a foot above the normal surface will change the appearance without costing a great deal.

Corner plantings and even doorway and foundation plantings may be used in the private area. A patio or porch, screened from the service area, can form part of your curved design. Near it you might have a small accent planting of flowers or shrubs or a display tree—perhaps even a potted tree or shrub.

A sports area or vegetable garden, or space devoted to any other special interest, will be part of the living area. The two I have mentioned are not very attractive, so they are generally separated from the rest of the yard by fencing or shrubs.

Your imagination, energy, and finances are the limiting factors in the designing of this area. It must please you—but only you!

The actual purchase of plants should also be a deliberate process. I recommend seeking advice from a nurseryman or a horticultural extension agent to be sure of selecting the correct types of plants for particular spots. Then, of course, they must be properly maintained.

*

INDEX

END OF VOLUME

Notes

Notes